HAUNTED CARLOW

HAUNTED CARLOW

Cormac Strain & Danny Carthy

The History Press Ireland

First published 2011

The History Press Ireland
119 Lower Baggot Street
Dublin 2
Ireland
www.thehistorypress.ie

© Cormac Strain & Danny Carthy, 2011

The right of Cormac Strain & Danny Carthy to be identified as
the Authors of this work has been asserted in accordance with the
Copyrights, Designs and Patents Act 1988.

All rights reserved. No part of this book may be reprinted
or reproduced or utilised in any form or by any electronic,
mechanical or other means, now known or hereafter invented,
including photocopying and recording, or in any information
storage or retrieval system, without the permission in writing
from the Publishers.
British Library Cataloguing in Publication Data.
A catalogue record for this book is available from the British Library.

ISBN 978 1 84588 697 4
Typesetting and origination by The History Press
Printed in Great Britain
Manufacturing managed by Jellyfish Print Solutions Ltd

Contents

	Foreword	7
one	The White Lady of Staplestown Road	11
two	Clonegal Castle	17
three	A Cafe with Spirit	21
four	The House with the Friendly Ghost	27
five	The Voices of Leighlinbridge	35
six	Brown Street Ghost Story	47
seven	A Paranormal Investigation	53
eight	The Phantom Worker	61
nine	The Students and the Poltergeist	69
ten	The Old Woman	77
eleven	The Banshee	81
twelve	County Carlow Tales	89

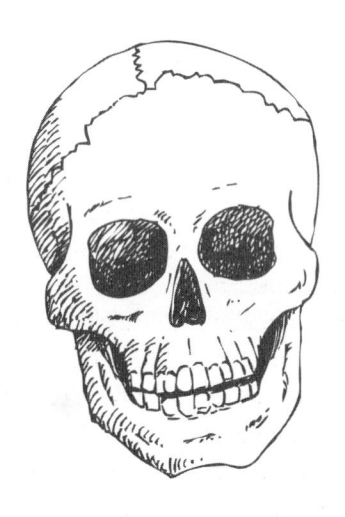

Foreword

I'VE never seen a ghost, have you? I've certainly had enough chances, spending over twenty years investigating allegedly haunted locations. But I'm not a ghostbuster; I'm a parapsychologist. Parapsychology is traditionally referred to as the scientific study of the paranormal. The paranormal phenomena studied by parapsychologists are traditionally divided into two branches: ESP (Extra Sensory Perception) and PK (Psychokinesis). ESP is a collective term for three alleged processes: telepathy (mind-to-mind interaction); clairvoyance (mind-to-object interaction), and precognition (mind-to-future interaction). PK is the movement of objects using the mind (such as spoon bending).

The area of parapsychology that I research, however, is the quite broad area of 'After Death Communication' (ADC), which could be witnessing apparitions of the dead (or haunting experiences generally) or the interaction of a medium with departed personalities (in a séance setting, one-to-one with a client, or in an alleged haunted house). This latter form of paranormal communication is seen as analogous to telepathic communication and, hence, comes under the remit of parapsychologists. Despite this, in the world today you would probably find only a handful of genuinely qualified parapsychologists who study such phenomena, who go out into allegedly haunted locations or observe mediums in their natural environments. It is because of this connection, and the many, many, *many* evenings spent listening to the screams of the *Most Haunted* team or the whisper of malevolent taps, that I'm privileged to have been asked to provide a foreword for this journey through Carlow's supernatural scenery.

Cormac and Danny present us with plenty of haunting and compelling stories, such as the hidden historical secrets of Carlow Shopping Centre or 'the old Carlow Gaol' and the fabulous traditional story of the Banshee given a new twist in a tale from Tullow. The accounts are peppered with wry humour, which, for a moment, gives that well-timed relief before a ghoulish surprise brings us back to the gothic atmosphere of a book of ghost stories. I couldn't help but smile at the image of Mark, an eyewitness, creeping downstairs after hearing noises at night, 'armed with a stout stick ... invaded the kitchen like a ninja'. It's the sort of reaction I've heard before, but the dramatic retelling of this, and many other eyewitness accounts had me gripped. I was also hooked reading about the poltergeist incidents, especially as a parapsychologist.

Poltergeist phenomena are commonly defined, in parapsychology, as 'displays of energy that induce movement of objects which are ordinarily held in place by inertia and gravity'. It is a word derived from German, meaning, literally, 'noisy spirit' (*poltern* – noisy, *geist* – spirit), and phenomena can also include loud noises, the appearance of water, apports and asports, and even spontaneous fires. Parapsychologists also refer to poltergeist phenomena as 'recurrent spontaneous psychokinesis' or RSPK. The reason for this is recognition of potential causes of the phenomena as being more to do with the living people in a location, rather than spirits. William Roll, the parapsychologist best known for researching poltergeist cases, feels that poltergeist events reflect psychological tension between a central person involved in the case and others, including, perhaps, investigators.

The idea that poltergeist activity is centred solely on a young girl, often a teenager, has been aided, in no small part, by the popular film of 1982. In *Poltergeist*, a family are plagued by the movement of household objects (like kitchen chairs) and apparitions, before being confronted with an apparent door 'to the other side'. The implication is that the activity is focused on Carol Anne, the youngest daughter in the family. There is a commonly held belief that pubescent girls are the catalyst for such events. The idea originates from late nineteenth-century psychical researchers. Households at that time would have been comprised of large families and it is no surprise that when rowdy, undetermined disturbances occurred, the clear culprits would be the youngsters with uncontrollable energy and prankish tendencies. Indeed, poltergeist research is plagued by discovery of fraud and trickery.

It is rare to find cases in which the multitude of exciting phenomena poltergeists are said to produce actually occur. As well as the usual 'raps, taps, thumps, thuds, crashes, bangs and bombinations' so poetically phrased by the renowned investigator/researcher Alan Gauld, there could also be the movement of objects, musical instruments playing, fires, the deluge of water, interference with electrical equipment, clothes tearing, etc. It's rare to find a case where all these things happen. Indeed, many of you may have experienced simple taps or thumps (check the water pipes!), or the movement of objects (try and capture it on film!), but to have experienced everything from paranormal arson to clothing vandalism would be truly out of this world! It was, therefore, fascinating to hear about a poltergeist case based in Carlow, reported directly to the authors, that had not just one type of phenomena, but a whole gamut, from objects moving and extreme temperature drops to tapping or clicking (from various sources) and lights mysteriously going on and off.

Cormac and Danny do not tread the well-worn path of many ghostly guides by recounting the oft-heard stories associated with well-known Carlow locations. They also give some of the locations a very personal edge. Whether it's an intimate reference to their own visit or simply retelling an experience of a friend, this more personal touch to the guide makes the reader feel they are getting something extra, and that I found fascinating. Fascinating because I never tire of hearing people's haunting experiences, and the collection here of encounters with dark figures or spine-chilling screams is no exception. As you take this journey round the weird and wonderful side of Carlow with Cormac and Danny, marvel in hidden treasures that they have discovered and that we, as readers, also discover. As someone who has been involved in haunting investigations and experiences for over two decades, I'm still amazed at the wealth of ghostly reports and haunted locations still out there. I'm grateful to Cormac and Danny for showing some more to us.

To finish, I'd like to turn to the words of Elliott O'Donnell, Irish author and ghost hunter. He's renowned in the world of 'ghost hunting' and he wrote many books based on his encounters with eye-witnesses and his own experiences; books that tell wild tales of almost-medieval ghosts and spirits, all with well-rounded narratives attached to them. His words capture mine and reflect the excitement I felt in reading about new stories, new locations and, ultimately, hearing about a place steeped in the supernatural that I'm now dying to visit:

'I think locality exercises strange influence over some minds. The peaceful meadow-scenery holds no lurking horrors in its bosom, but in the lonesome moorlands, full of curiously moulded boulders, grotesque fancies must assail one there. Creatures seem to come, odd and ill-defined as their surroundings. As a child I had a peculiar horror of those tall, odd-shaped boulders, with seeming faces, featureless, it is true, but sometimes strangely resembling humans and animals …'

Dr Ciarán O'Keeffe, 2011

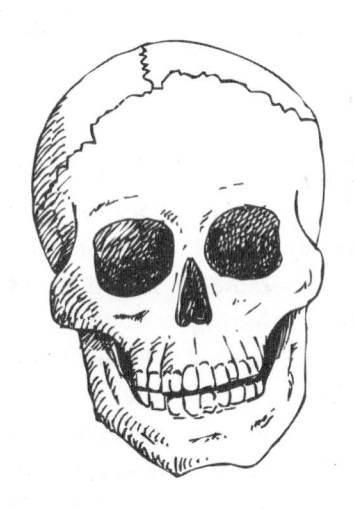

1
The White Lady of Staplestown Road

IN the early 1950s, local man Tom Hegarty was on his way home from the town and was walking along the Staplestown Road. Tom worked as a barman, and it was late in the evening as he made his way home to bed. The Staplestown Road of the 1950s wasn't like it is today; it wasn't as built up and even had a few fields alongside it. Roughly where Clayton Hall now stands, Tom noticed a young lady, in an immaculate white dress, standing at the side of the road. He gave her a cheery smile and a wave. She glared back at him. It was late at night, and Tom was a gentleman, so once again he tried to be cheery, saying, 'How you getting on Ma'am?' Once again he was met with an icy glare. He also noticed that this lady seemed to swivel around, always looking directly at him, even as he drew alongside her on the opposite side of the street. She had also been looking directly at him as he had approached her from further down the street, but he didn't see her move. It was a bit like looking at a picture with staring eyes – no matter where in the room you go, the picture still stares at you.

Tom was getting a little concerned for the lady's welfare. He never noticed her around Carlow before. She was very well dressed, it was late at night, and she looked like a respectable lady and not a hard-drinking floozie – so what was she doing glaring angrily at him like this at such a late hour? He decided to cross the road and find out what the problem was. That initially appeared to be a great plan …

Tom strode across the road, calling out to the lady, asking if she was OK. In response, she seemed to move further away in the opposite direction – but she didn't seem to physically move and she was still glaring angrily at Tom. Behind her was a field, and on the boundary between the pathway and field there was a stout fence. Tom, seeing that the lady was sure to collide with the fence, called out a warning. Two things – two inexplicable things – happened in quick succession. First, the lady glided through the fence itself. Tom stopped dead in his tracks. Then, as he was still recovering

Robert saw an 'ethereal fabric' on the top level of the bridge. © Fran McCormack, 2010.

from this shock, the lady in white just vanished in front of him. According to Tom, he can't remember how he got home. He was in complete shock. He did mention it to a few people over the following weeks, but the ridicule he received in return meant he didn't tell another soul until he came across our quest for Carlow ghost stories. Tom hadn't even heard the other tales of the Staplestown Road that we'd come across.

To be honest, as we carried out our research, we didn't immediately realise the number of stories there were about the Staplestown Road – all of which seem eerily similar. This next tale was told to us by a young man called Robert:

'The old pedestrian back lane which runs from the railway bridge on Staplestown Road up to Springdale was said by other children to be the haunting ground of the Banshee – a fairy woman, a messenger of death from the Otherworld. This lane also had a pathway at the top, leading you under another railway bridge and into New Oak Estate. The Banshee was said to have trailed up and down the lane at night, or sat lurking under the railway bridge at the New Oak Estate entrance, waiting for lone walkers.

Over the years I had frequently walked through the lane, from either entrance, during the day and night. All I ever saw at night were teenagers drinking beers and puffing cigarettes under the shelter of the bridge at the estate.

However, back in 1993 I did see something otherworldly in the vicinity. It was evening – still daylight but approaching dusk. The sky was dull with cloud and I was walking down Staplestown Road towards the town centre. I was on the opposite side of the road from St Killian's Crescent and could see McDarby's (now Spar) straight ahead, beyond the railway bridge.

Something caught my eye and I looked up. I saw a figure on the bridge, misty and greyish. It stood at the railings over the centre of the road. It was tall, but slender enough to assign it a female gender (if one had to be assigned). However, it had no defining physical attributes or facial features. It looked like it was draped with an ethereal fabric and long, wispy, hanging hair.

I realised the figure was looking in my direction and, as I continued walking, I kept looking at it to try and make sense of it. I noticed there were no eyes on its face, but dark patches or impressions instead. Its head tilted toward me as I walked down the slope toward the bridge, and I realised I was the focus of its attention. It was staring intently at me. I also realised no other person or motorist was on the road at the time. It was as if time stood still for these few moments.

Staplestown Road bridge, where Maura met a 'human-shaped cloud'.
© Fran McCormack, 2010.

Now blocked off to the public, the scene of Darragh's frightening Banshee experience. © Fran McCormack, 2010.

Then, the figure just vanished in the blink of an eye. I was not unnerved but felt rather curious and I hoped to see it again. I never did. Nobody I knew died prior to, or soon after, this incident.'

Interestingly, we had already tracked down a very similar story, but it was from twenty years before. In the early 1970s, a lady called Maura was walking from the town centre, down the Staplestown Road. Now in her mid-sixties, Maura told us much the same story, except the figure she saw was on the roadway, under the bridge:

'It was a bitter evening, and I was making my way towards the bridge, when, in the distance, I could see someone standing on the roadway below it. It was raining, so I assumed it was someone standing in out of the rain. It was only as I got nearer that I realised I couldn't make out anything more than a rough shape. I even stopped walking for a minute, as I thought I was looking at a human-shaped fog of some kind, before putting it down to the rain on my glasses obstructing my view. I was no more than ten yards away when it became very, very clear that there was a person there – but at the same time, there wasn't a person there. It was like a human-shaped cloud under the bridge. I stopped again, and as I did, the shape just vanished.'

Our two witnesses had never met nor talked to each other, yet both had almost the exact same story to tell. Though not the same story as the White Lady, could it be that time can change a ghost from a clearly defined figure to something 'draped with an ethereal fabric' or 'like a human-shaped cloud'?

Our final Staplestown Road witness, Darragh, brings a new twist to the tale:

'It would be almost twenty-five years ago now, when myself and the lady who is now my wife were walking under the railway bridge between New Oak Estate up to Springdale, on our way home. As we turned and walked parallel to the bridge, we both heard what I can only describe as the strangest, weirdest and creepiest kind of long, drawn-out, part moan, part scream and part cry – all three sounds seemed to happen at the same time. It was very loud, very clear and seemed to be coming from above on the bridge itself. This lasted for about a minute or so and we both stopped dead in our tracks – we could only look at each other. After it stopped I said, "Did you hear that?" to which my girlfriend, in jest, replied, "Sure that's only the Banshee." We had a laugh at that, and to be honest, I didn't really think any more of it. After all, it could have been a stray cat or a fox. It was only after my cousin died tragically in a car accident two weeks later that I remembered what we'd heard that night. The idea that it was a Banshee didn't seem so funny anymore.'

So just who or what occasionally visits the Staplestown Road? As far as we are aware, there haven't traditionally been any ghost stories associated with the road (though our second story does hint that there were local rumours of such things). Yet here are four individuals over a forty-year time span who seem to have had some very similar experiences. It makes one wonder just how many other people may have had similar experiences, but, like Tom, decided it best to keep such encounters to themselves for fear of ridicule.

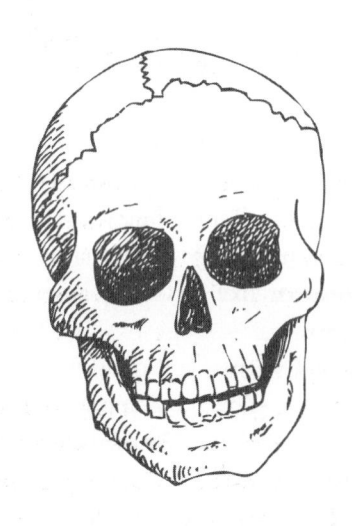

2

The Fellowship of Isis (FOI)

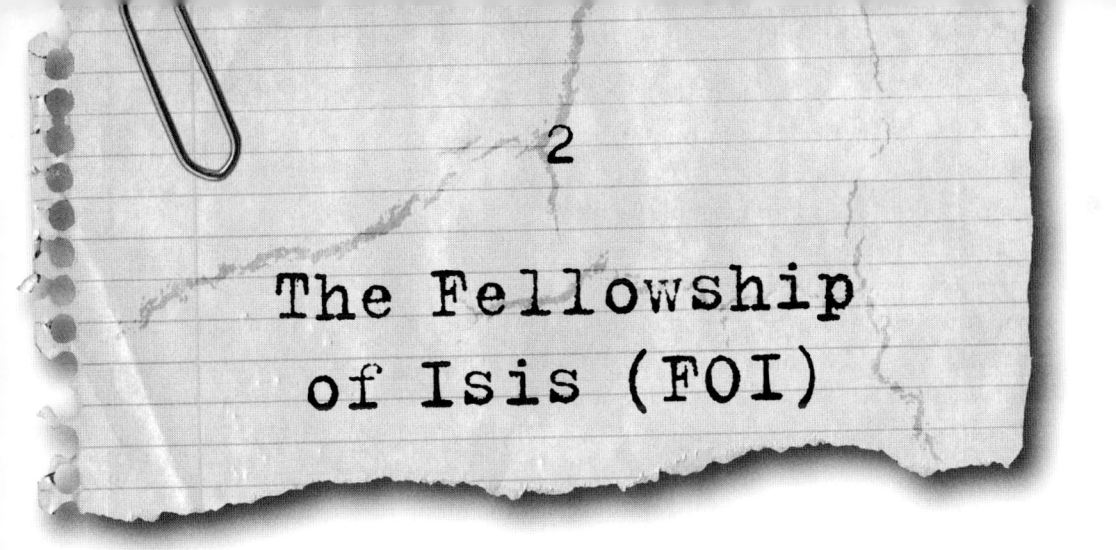

IN the far south-east of County Carlow, in a small village called Clonegal (Irish: *Cluain na nGall*, meaning 'Meadow of the Foreigners'), lies what is probably one of the county's most hidden treasures, Clonegal Castle (formerly known as Huntington Castle).

Clonegal Castle was built in 1625 (though some reports say it's from the fourteenth century), but fifty-five years later, in 1680, the castle name was changed from Clonegal to Huntington, by the then owner, Sir Laurence Esmonde. The Esmondes originally came from Hunnington in Lincolnshire, so it's assumed that the name 'Huntington' was due to a mispronunciation. It was changed back to its old name of Clonegal Castle in the 1970s. It was originally build for defensive purposes during the early seventeenth-century English plantation of the area. Cromwell captured the castle, because of its strategic importance and location on the Dublin–Wexford road, as he marched on Kilkenny in 1650. Some claim that the castle is built on ruins dating back to Druid times.

Clonegal Castle is certainly a mysterious place. Even its location has a celestial air about it, here described by Olivia Robertson, co-founder of the Fellowship of Isis and owner of the castle:

'Clonegal Castle lies on the banks of the River Derry (Doire, 'The Grove of the Oak'), upstream before it joins the Slaney (Slainte, 'River of Healing'). Matriarchal centres were situated between the two rivers on the Crow's Foot, the Macha (Crone form of the goddess Morrigan). Such is the site of Castle Matrix, where dwelt the Wizard Earl of Desmond. The confluence of our two rivers gives the name to our village Clonegal – Cluan i Gabhla, named after Eithne of the Long Fork.'

It may well seem very strange in this day and age to talk about witches, but that's precisely what we are now going to talk about. Witches. Real ones. In Carlow.

Clonegal Castle is the home of a worldwide organisation called the Fellowship of Isis (FOI). The Fellowship of Isis was founded at the Spring Equinox of 1976 at Clonegal Castle in Ireland, by Olivia Robertson, her brother Lawrence, and his wife, Pamela Durdin-Robertson, and has had an internet site since the very early days of the web – 1995. Dedicated specifically to the Egyptian goddess Isis, the FOI is a multifaith, multiracial, and multicultural organisation, and despite worshipping pagan deities, it does not consider itself to be a Neopagan faith.

The rites, ordinations, and mysteries of the FOI are performed in the Temple of Isis, which occupies the entire basement area of Clonegal Castle. It is approached through a double door in the hall at the rear of the castle, complete with two temple guardians with swords, originally from a Buddhist temple in Burma, and above which is a powerful mask of Neith, the Egyptian goddess of war and hunting. The shrines at Clonegal Castle are located in the lower level and are known collectively as 'The Temple of Isis'. Twenty-six shrines are set in a winding pattern throughout the main sanctuary. Within the chapel is a nave, a high altar and a chapel of Brigid, which is situated near a Neolithic well named Brigid's Well. The water of this well is famous for its healing properties. There are also twelve shrines dedicated to the signs of the Zodiac and five chapels dedicated to the magical elements of earth, air, fire, water and spirit. All in all a pretty ancient place – and we haven't even touched on the ghosts yet.

As if featuring in Discovery Channel's *Castle Ghosts of Ireland* and Stanley Kubrick's 1975 period film *Barry Lyndon* isn't enough, the pews in the chapel were apparently made for and given to the fellowship by the sister of Brigitte Bardot. Olivia says:

'In our Temple of Isis, my aim is to create rituals that teach the laws of expanding consciousness. These dramas aren't ritual magic in the practical sense, and they aren't intended to produce effects on the physical environment. Rather, they're meant to affect the minds and feelings of those taking part in group participation. For what is life as we know it but a group dreaming? And the drama of Isis and Osiris is about awakening into who we really are.'

Deep within the castle lies what is known as a sacred well, which has magical powers. In the history of the castle, this small, approximately fifteen-foot deep, well, which is said to be pre-Christian, has never run dry, even in times of siege. Outside, along the boundaries of the castle, are areas where fairies apparently roam, including the Fairy Seat in the river. As Olivia describes it, 'The cave was naturally formed by a gigantic rock split down the middle in a chasm. Rain water formed a deep stream that emerged from a black tunnel. I looked into the dark tunnel and knew there was a fairy portal to the underworld.'

There is, however, much more to Clonegal Castle than the Fellowship of Isis, mysterious ancient wells and fairies; 'Disturbing apparitions' is how the Discovery Channel put it. An eyewitness reports seeing robed figures regularly crossing a field adjacent to the castle – robed figures which then vanished before his eyes.

Then there's poor Ailish. Sir Esmonde, himself a Protestant, was married to Ailish O'Flaherty, who was decidedly Catholic. It was obviously a marriage of convenience, as was fashionable at the time, because one night Ailish stole off to her family in Connacht with baby son Thomas. Sir Esmonde does not seem to have been overly concerned, and he merrily went off and got himself another wife. The Banshee-like wraith that has, on occasion, been witnessed on the lawns, has been ascribed to Ailish, 'combing her long hair by the moonlight and wailing in grief-stricken anguish at the unfairness of it all', according to Carlow writer and historian Turtle Bunbury. As with many such stories, though, there are variations. Some believe that she is waiting anxiously for the return her husband and son who went off to the wars. But this seems like a weird thing to do if she had left the castle with her son when he was a babe in arms.

The late David Durdin-Robertson reported having a strange vision in the castle library when he was a teenager. Reading in the library one afternoon, with his father Laurence. He nodded off on the couch, only to awaken in a much brighter room, 'I woke up to see two faces staring down at me.' At this stage, David himself started to float up off the couch towards the two faces, 'It was a most extraordinary experience. They hadn't touched me – they just looked down at me and it was as if I was in their power.' It seems to have been a bit of an out-of-body experience, where David could observe himself as he floated.

Some claim that this may be leftover energy from the druids, who, it is said, occupied the site on which Clonegal Castle now stands. With these claims also come those of ancient human sacrifice and the deaths of those who continue to haunt Clonegal Castle to this day. One troupe of ghosts seems to only appear at night and comprises figues quite similar to those witnessed walking through the surrounding fields during the day. On the grounds of Clonegal Castle are the ruins of what was an ancient abbey, including a very old canopy of yew trees, reputedly more than 700 years old. Over the years, among these trees, many people believe they have seen a procession of monks, solemnly walking in the darkness, before silently vanishing. Others claim that these aren't monks at all, but in fact the ancient druids.

As with any building of such standing and age, there have been deaths associated with the castle. In the Jacobean hall in 1738, the young Richard Esmonde died from 'accidental discharge of his fowling piece'. There are no direct reports of Richard haunting the castle, but there is the phantom who knocks on the main door. It's believed to be a spectral soldier, thought to have lived in the seventeenth century, during Cromwell's rebellion. In life, he disguised himself in the uniform of the opposition in order to spy on the enemy, but tragically his comrades didn't recognise him as he returned to the castle and they shot him through the grille of the door, where his ghostly face is now sometimes seen.

Not content with Banshee-like wraiths in the garden, floating spirits in the library and phantom soldiers knocking on doors, Clonegal Castle even has its own lady phantoms haunting its corridors. Barbara St Leger and her maidservant Honor Byrne, we are told, frequent the corridors to the sound of jangling keys, while polishing door handles with their hair. It's a wonder no one has ever thought to leave out a few dishcloths for them!

Revd James Leslie – he of another famous Irish Castle, Castle Leslie, as well as Bishop of Limerick – visited Clonegal Castle for a brief spell in 1770. Considering he apparently died in the castle, 'brief' is probably the wrong word, but there are those who claim to have seen the apparition of the sizeable bishop in the Four Poster Room, where it is said he shuffled off this mortal coil. Unfortunately it has proven almost impossible to track down any such witnesses, but again, considering the reports have spanned a period of over 200 years, maybe this isn't so surprising. Another bedroom in the building claims to have done quite a bit of mortal-coil shuffling, with thirteen people having died in it. Maybe, over the period of 400-odd years, thirteen isn't an exceptional amount, but in fairness it's a scary number.

Funnily enough, maybe not all the ghosts at Clonegal Castle were actually dead. Olivia tells an entertaining story concerning her uncle, who, as she explains, fell out of favour with the family:

'All my mother would say evasively, when I enquired, was 'If anyone mentions your uncle, say it was shellshock!' I gathered he had committed three offences.

The first was that he had become a Roman Catholic. The second was that he openly admitted voting for De Valera (Republican). The third could not be mentioned at all, as it was wicked. Oscar Wilde had done it. So my uncle was forbidden ever to come home to the castle. His own mother, my grandmother, repudiated him. She was a very religious Anglican.

How did my rejected uncle cope? He did manage to get back to his beloved home. How? He became a ghost. No, he did not kill himself. He was still alive. But he used to come for lengthy periods to live in hiding in the wing. I had heard of the Monster of Glamis and Jane Eyre, but my uncle looked alright – good-looking and normal in fact.

Our family did not ever enter the wing, but it was next to the staff quarters. Our good-hearted butler used to keep my uncle alive with trays of food. Exercise? That was taken care of. He used to come out at night and glide through our wilderness and by the river. And this was where he became the 'Castle Ghost'. For many a brave citizen of Clonegal would spy him amidst the trees at night. They would return and tell fascinated listeners, 'I saw the ghost of the poor gentleman by the lake, all pale and thin.' He would sometimes be sighted by the River Derry, once used by the Druids, or making his ghostly way down the haunted Yew Walk, where monks made phantom procession.'

It just shows that you can never really tell with Clonegal Castle; is it haunted or is it just full of history?

3

A Cafe with Spirit

MENTION the word 'ghosts' in Carlow Town and someone is bound to say 'the old Carlow Gaol'. It has enticed paranormal research groups to spend nights there, local radio station KCLR to host a fright night there, and even to play host to RTÉs *Baz's Culture Clash*. Carlow Gaol is one of those places where it seems someone opened a large box of history and stuffed it into the building ... creating a few hauntings along the way.

Carlow Gaol is now Carlow Shopping Centre, plumb in the middle of the town. It has an incredible history. Built in 1800, the gaol replaced the older County Bridewell, where many United Irishmen were held (the 1798 gaol stood across the road from the modern-day shopping centre). Many believe the apparent hauntings of Carlow Shopping Centre originate from its time as a gaol.

When originally built, Carlow Gaol centred around the four-storey Governor's House (which is now Cafe le Monde) and surrounding this was the matron's house, thirty female prisoner cells and thirty-five male prisoner cells, all enclosed by a twenty-foot high granite wall. The centrepiece of the wall was the impressive entrance, which remains but now leads people into the shopping centre rather than the murky insides of a prison – a journey that many times in the distant past used to be one-way only.

It's worth taking a good look at this entrance if you ever get the chance. Look closely at the window over the gate and beneath it you will see where a horizontal slot has been filled with mortar. This was where a wooden platform with a trap door was pushed out – hard to believe, but true. If you look at the keystone in the arch above, you will see a slot where the 'Gibbet' was fixed; all that would have been missing was the unfortunate prisoner, and Carlow Gaol had a seemingly inexhaustible supply of those. The trap door is now in the museum in Carlow.

The Treadmill and Debtors' Prison were on the Barrack Street side of the gaol. Prisoners worked the treadmill,

Cafe le Monde and the main area of Carlow Shopping Centre. © Fran McCormack, 2010.

which pumped water from a well for use in the gaol. During reconstruction work in 1840 or 1853, part of the Old Carlow Wall was discovered in Potato Market near the gaol.

Quite a few people were executed at the gaol for various crimes, many of which were brought about by poverty and hunger. Others – like Lucy Sly's murder of her husband – were not so innocent. Sly waited until her man was asleep, then, handing a hatchet to her apparent lover, John Dempsey, made sure that Walter Sly never awoke again. Then they took the body outside to the stables and shot it to make it look like robbery. The following is taken from a report of the court case:

One man who knew the Slys and wasn't afraid to speak out was the Revd John Doyne. When examined by the Crown he was quite forthright in his testimony.

'I knew Sly about twelve years and I knew his wife for the same time.' About five years ago she complained to me of the ill-treatment she received from her husband. He was a man of a most violent temper. She told me that upon occasion she was turned out without any clothing at night, and beaten with a horsewhip.'

Another of Walter's neighbours, Mr Robert Phillips, Esq., was made executor of Walter's will. He testified that in the will dated 16 January 1827, Walter, with the exception of a small legacy to his nephew, left all his property to his wife, Lucinda. Mr Phillips also saw the deceased's body on the Sunday morning and the pistol that was found the following Monday. 'It was locked up in Sly's chest,' said Mr Phillips. Referring to Lucinda, he said:

'I called for the key, and she replied she had no key to open it. She then said that Sly brought the key with him to the fair; I insisted on getting a key. I examined her person and found two keys, the first of which I took opened the chest freely. The keys now produced are the same as those found. Her son, Thomas Singleton, produced a second key which he said belonged to Sly. It opened the chest also. I found the pistol. Captain Battersby and the police were present. I examined the pistol; it was loaded as if a person were in a hurry or in confusion; the cartridge was not driven home. It was primed, and had the appearance of being recently discharged.'

Lucinda Sly was executed by hanging in Carlow Gaol. Many, including Dominic Peel, proprietor of Cafe le Monde, which is currently located in the Governor's House, believe Lucy is behind many of the poltergeist-like activities witnessed in the cafe itself and in the centre in general. Dominic explains:

'We opened here in 1995, and during the time we were fitting out the premises we heard all kinds of stories of the place being haunted and the history of the place, but during those three months of preparation we had no inkling of anything strange.

The first experience was during our first week of business. A friend of mine, who had a restaurant in Waterford, rang me to say he had friends coming up to Carlow and to ask if I would look after them. I said that I would of course and that the best thing to do would be to give them a letter just to state who they were. The people duly arrived with the letter and had some lunch. I asked the cashier to keep the letter in the till and to write the end bill value on it when the guests had finished. Obviously, at the end of the night, when the cashiers were accounting their tills, there was a shortfall which matched the value of the guests' meal that day – but there was no sign of the signed letter anywhere. I wasn't too perturbed by this; it was a small amount of money, which I would be redeeming off my restaurant friend anyway, so I thought no more of it.

One evening, about a week later, when it came to totting up the tills, we were all quite surprised to find the A4-sized letter in the same till. The letter hadn't been in the till during the day, nor had anyone seen it at all during the previous week, but all of a sudden it seemed to reappear in the same place from which it had disappeared.

That was the first experience, and to be honest we didn't think much about it, but from there on things began to happen. For example, every Friday, late in the afternoon, we'd get a dry goods order in from our supplier (dry goods being flour, beans, tinned food, etc.). On one particular Friday, the order arrived in at 5 p.m., just as our chef's shift was ending. Since she was in the next morning, the chef decided to leave packing away the order until then. As these were dry goods, they wouldn't require refrigeration or anything of that nature so there was no harm in leaving them where they were until the next day.

But when she came in the next morning everything was done. Now this wasn't a five-minute job; this was something that would have taken quite a bit of time to do. And so our chef assumed the manager on duty had organised some staff to put away the dry goods, so off she went to find the manager and say thanks. The only problem was that the manager hadn't organised any staff to pack away the goods. No one had even been in the kitchen area before the chef had arrived. To this day, we don't know how the dry goods got packed away.

Another similar event occurred one night after the staff mopped the floors at the end of business. They stacked the chairs on the tables, which obviously made the job easier, and the chairs would stay on the tables until the next morning, when the floor had properly dried. On this particular occasion, the next morning the chairs were arranged properly around the tables. But at this stage we were getting used to these kinds of strange things happening, so even though we knew none of us had taken the chairs off the tables, we weren't too concerned at the same time. It was a bit freaky all the same.'

The strange happenings were not confined to poltergeist-like experiences in the gaol, however. Dominic went on to say that other members of his staff have had some more startling experiences:

'It was a Friday night and we were open late – this would have been around 1995/6. The manager and three or four other staff would have been rostered to close up shop at the end of the shift, and since the cafe staff would have cleaning chores at the end of every working day, our staff would be the last to leave the shopping centre itself. When they were finished, our staff would switch off the lights, lock up, arm the security system and leave.

I arrived back at work the following morning and checked with the cafe manager about any issues or problems from the late shift the night before. She reported that there had been no problems, bar that the light in the boiler room (in the attic) had obviously been left on, as they could see it shining from the top of the old Governor's house (the present-day cafe) just as they were going out the door. Rather than unarming the alarm and going back into the building, she decided to leave the light until that morning, and switched it off when she started work that day. Alarm bells started ringing in my head right away, as there

What used to be the crèche when the centre opened was the scene of some paranormal activity © Fran McCormack, 2010.

is only one light in the attic, which is in the boiler room itself. The window in the boiler room is blocked off and the boiler room itself is, for health and safety reasons, completely blocked off from the rest of the attic, bar a heavy fire door, so there is no way that anyone could actually see that light from outside – it is a closed-off room. The light the staff had seen could not have come from the only light source in the attic. Even if the fire door had been open, the light couldn't have been seen from outside.

Intrigued, I went up to the attic myself to double check everything. The light in the boiler room was off, but curiously, the fire door was wedged open with a very old, flat, almost triangular-shaped nail. I'd never seen a nail like it before, but since first and foremost it was against protocol to have the fire door open like that, I marched downstairs to demand an explanation from the manager as to who had jammed open the door and why. She was just as surprised as I was to this development, as she had firmly closed the door earlier that morning when she had turned off the light. Access to the attic is beside the manager's office upstairs, and the stairs to the attic are very creaky and noisy, so the manager was quite adamant that no one had been in the attic after she had left it, considering she had been in her office all morning and would easily have heard anyone going up there. Don't forget, the door wasn't just left open (it's a spring loaded door anyway), it was wide open and wedged with a flat nail so it didn't happen by accident.

I've since found that these flat nails were called "square nails" and first came into use in the end of the eighteenth century. These days they are only used in antique renovations, and certainly none had been used in the redevelopment of the shopping centre and Cafe le Monde. The prime production period of these nails was between 1820 and 1910. Maybe it's from the old woodwork here and got dislodged during renovations, but that doesn't explain how it was firmly wedged under the door.'

As a side note, while researching this book we heard of a security guard who, in 2005, had much the same experience. While doing his rounds in the centre, he too noticed a light on in the attic of the cafe, and reported it to staff the following day. Unfortunately we couldn't track down that particular security guard to confirm, but it does seem to back up Dominic's account. Dominic continued:

There are other reports of noises in the area of the office. I have personally on many occasions heard the door outside the office opening and closing as if someone is coming in, but when I'd check there'd be no one there, nor anyone in the upstairs area at all. This still happens – it's almost a daily occurrence. It can't be the wind, as the door – like all doors in the centre – is spring loaded. I've just got used to it, though I do still check if anyone has come upstairs. Nine times out of ten, no one has.

As Frank Carson used to say, 'and there's more ...':

'About the time we opened, the staff from the crèche arrived for work, opened the crèche door and found the toys scattered all over the floor. There's only way into the crèche and that's through the centre itself, so it's still a mystery as to how the toys had been flung around the place.

Such things don't happen as much these days as they did when we first opened – it was like the ghost was just introducing itself to us and letting us know it's here – but periodically odd occurrences do continue to happen within the centre.'

4

The House with the Friendly Ghost

There are parts of the Carlow border which neighbouring Laois may lay claim to. So this is like one of those little 'may contain nuts' warnings, as someone reading this is bound to drop their copy of Haunted Carlow *in horror exclaiming, 'But this story may have taken place in Laois!' We have decided, therefore, that we won't give away the exact location. This should preserve your copy of* Haunted Carlow *from unnecessary damage!*

ON the outskirts of Carlow, in a small, remote townland, lies an old cottage. Built sometime in the 1940s, this cottage was originally a small, two-room affair built by the local council. Looking at it from the road, it's hard to imagine its walls harboured anything like a ghost. Set in a small plot of land, the place looks like a picture postcard of rural Ireland, with small but well-looked-after lawns to the front and rear, ivy on the walls and flowerbeds – lots of flowerbeds. It's the kind of place any young couple could see themselves living the rest of their lives in. It could be argued that if the auctioneer who brought one such young couple to view the property at the turn of the recent millennium had actually mentioned that the place came with its own friendly ghost, they might not have thought it the perfect home for their young family after all. Or maybe they still would have. The words 'friendly' and 'ghost' aren't two that normally go together, but to this day this is what this family insist their extra, invisible tenant was.

It was late 2001 when the Rourke family moved into their new home. Renovations had taken four months, as Roy and Kacy put their own mark onto this sixty-year-old building – something which previous tenants had also done. What had started as a small, two-room cottage had now expanded to include a bathroom, kitchen, living room and a few extra bedrooms. Along with their two young children, eight-year-old Noel and older brother Adrian (two years senior and something he constantly reminded his younger sibling of), the Rourkes adored their new home. 'It's something even the workmen during the renovation had commented on,' says Roy. 'The place just seemed so safe and comfortable – like it had its own guardian angel watching over the whole place.' It was this 'safe and comfortable' feeling that later acted as a buffer when first Roy, then Noel, and eventually the level-headed Kacy began to wonder if they weren't in fact, just going mad. Roy explains:

'I don't know when it started. I suppose the first thing I noticed would have been after a year or so when myself and Kacy were watching TV. I could have sworn I'd seen someone quickly walk past the window to the side of the house. I didn't really think much of it until Kacy got up, looked out and said, 'Who was that?' Any kind of ghost just didn't enter our heads. I went outside and searched around the house in case we had an intruder but didn't find anyone. With no other explanation, we assumed it was someone who, somehow and for some reason had been in our backyard. What else could we think?'

Though it obviously was a tad disturbing to have someone prowling around their backyard, there was no indication of the identity of the real culprit. It didn't start to make its presence felt for another few months. 'Initially, I seem to have been the person who seemed to witness a lot of the "activity". Nothing concrete – just enough to wonder for your sanity.' Roy is a bit of a night owl, normally staying up until the wee hours to catch up with his Sky+. It was during one of these nightly vigils that Roy realised that, although he would usually hear someone (which he had assumed to be one of the kids) walking up the hall and using the bathroom each night around 1 a.m., he never really heard anyone making the return journey from the bathroom back to their bedroom. It was only after a few months of this activity that he decided to start checking who it was making these nightly trips. Initially, it was the sound of someone walking up the hall, the sound of the bathroom door opening and then nothing. After ten minutes, Roy would poke his head out the door to the corridor, hear nothing but absolute silence, then check the bathroom to find it empty and everyone sound asleep in their beds. As intriguing as this may seem now, at the time Roy just assumed the person had left before he had checked. Eventually though, curiosity got the better of him, so it came to the point where the instant he heard the sound in the hallway and the bathroom door opening, he crept out to the hall (feeling, it has to be said, like a thief in his own home) to check the bathroom. Which was in darkness. With the door open. No one had been there and when he checked, everyone else in the house was fast asleep.

At times like this, the first thing that jumps to mind isn't necessarily, 'Oh no! Ghosties!' It's, 'Oh no! Am I going mad?' Roy could not make head nor tail of this. He sat down, mulled the whole thing over, finished his coffee (Roy is one of those strange creatures who can easily drink coffee and then sleep) and went off to bed – bemused more than anything else.

One weird experience does not a haunting make. Again, it was another few months before anything else untoward seemed to occur, and it was something that Roy didn't recall for a time afterwards as initially it didn't seem paranormal. This one-off occurrence was that Roy found little Noel in tears – half asleep but in tears. 'The bed is moving Daddy ...' was all he could manage to say through the sobbing. Now Roy is a pretty level-headed chap, and seeing that his son was in fact half asleep, he assured Noel it was nothing more than a dream and coaxed him back to sleep. It would be at least six months before Roy would realise that it wasn't a dream after all, as he told me as we talked in that same house:

'At the time I was working nightshifts. In fact, I feel uneasy talking about this here, in the house, but I was working nightshifts and arrived home around 4 a.m. I was absolutely knackered but when I got to our bedroom I found little Noel tucked in beside Kacy, fast asleep. Rather than moving him I decided I'd sleep in his room and so within five minutes I was in bed, with the lights off, settling down. The only thing on my mind was whether I should stay up a bit longer and try to reorganise my sleep pattern or just try and nod off there and then, but my thoughts were interrupted by quite a loud sighing coming from the middle of the room.'

This sighing didn't startle Roy, as he was deep in thought. It was only after he heard it that he had to double check:

An artist's impression: "At times like this, the first thing that jumps to mind isn't 'Oh no! Ghosties!' It's 'Oh no! Am I going mad?'"
© Fran McCormack, 2010.

'"What the hell was that?" I thought. Then I got the shivers as it dawned on me that I was the only person in the room and it wasn't me sighing. Again, I wondered more about my own sanity than the idea of a ghost. Either I was going mad or there was something else in the room, and I sided with the theory that I may in fact be losing the marbles. The idea of a ghost was just impossible.'

It must have come as a relief for Roy when he chided Noel the next morning:

'Obviously I wasn't going to say anything about my experience to my young son, but I gently teased to him for sleeping in his parents' bed when he was a big, strong eight year old. I swear, I almost dropped when he told me he couldn't get to sleep in that room that night as he kept hearing someone sighing. It was around this time I seriously started considering that maybe I wasn't actually going mad. If the place wasn't haunted then the house was built on a patch of land affected by some hallucinogenic gas. At this stage of the game, I just didn't know what was going on.'

What started as a trickle, turned into a flood:

'I was going to bed late one night and I couldn't find the alarm clock. I even turned on the light in the room to look, even though Kacy was fast asleep and I didn't want to wake her. It was important to find the clock as it was late and I had an early start in the morning, but I couldn't find it anywhere. Imagine my surprise when I awoke the next morning to the sound of the alarm clock, which was neatly placed on the pillow right beside my head. I did not put it there and Kacy was still asleep.'

It didn't end there:

'Really, when you experience these kinds of things, you honestly just don't know what to think. Could I prove there was a ghost just because of a few sighs and an alarm clock? The simple answer is no. By this time, just to be on the safe side, I used to "talk" to the house in my head. Don't forget, I wasn't too sure that I hadn't gone insane, so talking to the house didn't seem that odd to me at the time. Anyway, I basically just asked that if there was some presence in the house, to make itself known in some way – do something definitive, something that I could not doubt wasn't normal. Literally, about a week after this, early one Tuesday morning, Kacy went to open the door of the living room and the door feel flat inwards. In each door hinge, the metal bar that connects both sides had been fully drawn up, right to the edge. Not far enough for the bars themselves to fall out, but far enough, on both hinges, to separate the part on the door frame and the part on the door. As usual, I had been up late the night before and that door had worked just fine seven hours beforehand. I think it was around then that I realised that we did in fact have a ghost in the house, but one that didn't wish to intrude or to scare us. What did it want though?'

The ghost must have sensed that the family had noticed its presence, as its next appearance was an epic one. As Roy explains:

'Surreal is the word I'd use. All I remember is being woken up by Adrian really early one morning, 'Dad! Dad! What's that noise? Dad!' Right enough, I could hear loud music coming from the kitchen. At this stage the whole family was awake. It is just amazing how sleep affects the brain. When I think back, there's no way in hell I would march into

A stereo just like the one that switched itself on. © Fran McCormack, 2010.

the pitch-black kitchen like I did then, without a care in the world, but at the time, for some reason, I thought it was a normal morning around 7 a.m., and that we were all getting up as usual. I was half asleep. It was only when I focused on the hall clock, with my hand opening the kitchen door, that I realised that it was in fact 4 a.m. and that the radio in the kitchen was blaring. I had already opened the door at this stage and it was like I just woke up anew. I was now terrified as the kitchen was in darkness and the radio was really on full blast. More scarily, was it was a very simple radio with no timer, no alarm, no way at all that it could automatically turn itself on at random. It was also on top of the tallboy, putting it a good eight feet off the ground. Even if one of the kids had been sleepwalking, they would have needed a ladder to get at it. Kacy or I would normally stand on a chair to switch it on or off. I switched the radio off and hurriedly convinced the rest of the family it was an electrical fault. My only regret is that I didn't check the plug, as it was the norm for us to unplug the radio when not in use. At the same time, if it had been unplugged then it

31

An artist's impression: one weird experience does not a haunting make.
© Fran McCormac, 2010.

would have completely freaked me out, so maybe it was good I didn't check.'

A slew of strange happenings, but none that could be considering threatening. All except one:

'Again I was working late and when I got home, the bedroom light was on, the door was wide open, the blankets were all over the place and there was no sign of Kacy. The first place I checked was the kids' room, and lo and behold, there she was, fast asleep, cradling our youngest. I assumed Noel had woken up during the night and for whatever reason Kacy had to comfort him. I went off to bed and slept soundly. It was only the next day that I found out what had happened.'

Kacy takes up the story:

'Well, I was in bed reading a book when I heard someone whispering, 'Kacy!' My first thought was that I had drifted off to sleep, but as I was thinking this I heard it again, only this time a bit louder. Now this time I thought, 'I definitely heard that!' and no sooner had I thought that when I heard, 'KACY!' once more – this time much more urgent and much louder. I freaked out and literally leaped out of the bed and into the hallway. The blankets and all went flying in every direction. I just wanted to get out of that room, so I ran into the kids' room and jumped into the nearest bed and literally hid. It really scared me.'

Just what was going on in this little cottage? What did this ghost, spirit, call it what you will, actually want? This is where good old coincidence kicked in. Roy continued:

'I have no time at all for so-called mediums. I just don't go for the whole speaking-with-dead-people thing, and even now after all that happened I still find I can't really deal mentally with that idea. In saying that though, we had a medium in our house one evening, completely by accident.

If there is such a thing as ideal conditions in which to test a medium, then this was it. A good friend of ours from Australia rang our home number one evening. He and his wife were in Carlow for a month, having just landed a few days before. He had never seen our new house (though we'd been there for a few years at this stage). The only thing our friend had was our number, which we had taken with us from our old home. We didn't really know a lot about his wife and certainly didn't know anything about her being psychic, just as our friend had no idea about any of the strange occurrences around our home. We made plans to meet up and go for a meal, which we did. There was so much catching up to do, so after the meal we made our way back to our house for a coffee.'

Roy almost seems embarrassed as he gets to the whole 'medium' part of the story:

'Basically, we were only in the house for about five minutes when our friend's wife starts talking about someone connected to our house. I looked at our friend quizzically and we both went outside for a quick tête-à-tête. "Buddy," says our friend in his Aussie accent, "It's not something we talk a lot about, but my wife is psychic – has been all her life. She's not very fond of it and finds it a pain in the ass to be honest, but the way she sees it is sometimes she goes places and people want to pass on information. I know what it sounds like buddy – it took me years to get my head around it, but she's genuine."'

Roy shrugs with a 'what can you do?' type gesture:

'Our house has a history with one particularly tragic accident that took the life of one of the previous occupants. I honestly don't want to go into the details as relatives and family of the person still live in the area and it just wouldn't be right – but we already knew the details. Name, age, what had happened. This is the same information this woman came out with when describing who the 'ghost' was. Yet this woman came from Australia two days beforehand; she didn't know she would end up in our house and certainly didn't know where we lived until that evening. As far as I can make out, the tragedy itself happened while she and her husband were in Australia, so she couldn't have previous knowledge, even if, per chance, she happened to know the house, which itself is virtually impossible. She also asked us to pass on information to the family from the deceased. That was an awkward thing to do, believe you me, but we did pass on the info and were told that no one outside the family knew of it. I genuinely can't explain how this lady knew that information unless she really was talking to a dead person.'

So how does the story end? 'Well,' concludes Roy, 'since we had that conversation with the deceased family, all ghostly activity has stopped. No more sighing noises (we heard them on numerous occasions), no more banging and bumping noises at night, and thankfully no one whispering, "Kacy! Kacy! KACY!" and scaring the bejesus out of my wife!'

5

The Voices of Leighlinbridge

THERE are many beautiful areas within the county of Carlow, but one of the quaintest has to be Leighlinbridge. Found on the Carlow–Kilkenny border, it's here that our next story occurs.

In researching *Haunted Carlow*, we found our stories usually through one of two ways: we either got an email from a first-hand witness, or we heard of a story and then happily went of to try to track down the source. We struck gold with this one, as not only was the story we had heard identical to the witness's interview (that's always a good sign), but the people themselves were decent, honest and down to earth. This couple were actually a bit concerned that we had tracked them down, as they had no idea so many people knew of their experiences. Reactions like this always please us, as it's obvious the couple weren't looking for any kind of attention. Combine this with the similarity between the story we had initially heard and the account we got directly from the couple themselves, and you have an experience that's unbelievable but more than likely true.

Paul and Breda had only been married a few years and buying a house in Carlow was proving to be a pretty difficult task (as it was countrywide). House prices were astronomically high. After months of searching, the couple finally managed to find a house that was not only in their price range, but also what they still class as their 'dream home'.

Nestled in a leafy area just outside Leighlinbridge, the small cottage, with its neat garden and low wall, was precisely what they were after. It looked small but it had four bedrooms – plenty of room for a young family to grow into. Breda was expecting their first child, so the timing of their purchase and subsequent move was ideal. This place was heaven. The house was structurally sound and it was pretty old, dating back almost 120 years. It was absolute perfection and Breda was certain she would be happy in their new abode.

However, it didn't take too long to change Breda's mind. At first it wasn't too disturbing, which is how the most disturb-

Leighlinbridge. © Fran McCormac, 2010.

ing things tend to start. It was around 11 a.m. on a frosty January morning. Paul had left for work a few hours earlier and Breda – for a change – had the day to herself. They been in the cottage two months at this stage, and Breda had worked as hard as her condition would allow her, cleaning, tidying and coaxing the little cottage to look as good as it felt to live in. On this day she didn't feel up to it. Little Junior was getting pretty active and there weren't many months left before he or she would make a first appearance, so this January morning was going to be spent making coffee, reading a novel and generally relaxing.

Settling in, Breda suddenly heard her name called quite clearly in her left ear. It didn't help that she was just about to drink a mouthful of coffee at the same time. The coffee went up in the air and the mug went in the opposite direction, hitting the floor with a sharp crash. 'Damn it', thought Breda, convinced she'd nodded off to sleep. Falling asleep while about to take a sip of coffee would be a pretty fantastic parlour trick, but it was the best explanation Breda could come up with. It had to have something to do with being pregnant. 'That's the answer', she thought. Some women eat raw liver when expecting, so the odd mild hallucination isn't that bad.

On the kitchen table, Breda's phone started to ring. She picked it up to hear Paul asking, 'Everything OK, love?'

'Paul, have you turned psychic or something? I nodded off to sleep there and spilled my coffee but otherwise, I'm perfectly fine. What's up?'

'I was going to ask you the same thing', Paul responded, sounding a tad confused. 'Sure you didn't just ring me there about a minute ago? I answered, said hello, I heard you say my name and then you hung up. It was your name that came up on my phone anyway.'

You can imagine the conversation. Breda wasn't going to let pregnancy stretch things that far though. She may have heard her name being called, caused by nodding off to sleep, but she didn't phone Paul. At least she didn't think she did. No – it was an error with Paul's phone. 'You should send that phone of yours in to get checked somewhere Paul. It was obviously someone else ringing you and they got cut off, and for some reason your phone has logged it as a call from me. I told you a €20 phone bought at a market wouldn't be up to much.' Sometimes Paul's idea of saving money ended up costing more money, and his phone was obviously a shining example of this. After a bit of small talk, the call ended and Breda snuggled back down to reading her book. *Knock, knock, knock*, went the back door. 'Breda' came in a quiet whisper from somewhere in the same vicinity. Breda almost fell off the chair. There was no doubting it this time; someone just whispered her name … and knocked on the door. With a rush, Breda lurched for the back door and pulled it open wide. No one. She ran around the house, ran on to the lawn and scanned the road far in both directions. There was no one. 'If …', thought the logical part of Breda's brain, 'that's the case, then who the hell was knocking? And who had been whispering my name?' There was no response from the creative side of Breda's brain, as it was cowering in the corner, trying not to be noticed.

This time, in a panic, she really did ring Paul. Paul's first thought was that Breda was winding him up. It was only amidst his laughter, when she started to cry, that Paul realised that Breda was serious. He immediately left the office and started the twenty-minute drive home. Intruders, that's what Paul was worried about, not ghosts. Paul was normally a safe driver, but if there was an intruder lurking on his property Paul needed to get home to protect his wife. He cut his journey time in half. Pulling into the driveway, he could see Breda sitting out in the garden. 'I feel safer out here for the minute,' she told her husband. 'Whoever knocked on the door might still be around.'

The nearest neighbour was almost two miles away and the cottage was surrounded by fields. Maybe someone was playing silly buggers – though how someone could be cruel enough to frighten a heavily pregnant woman was something Paul couldn't fathom. Worse things do happen though, so thinking that someone may have run back into the fields, Paul started a dedicated search of the house and its immediate surroundings. There was no sign of anyone.

Putting it down to some kind of twisted prank, the couple went back into the house and tried to rearrange their plans for the day. It was lunchtime and Paul needed to return to work, but Breda wasn't interested in staying at the cottage on her own. She obviously didn't say this to Paul (it was their dream home after all) but she made excuses so she could spent the afternoon in Carlow, and Paul could collect her on his way back from work. Breda made a quick lunch before the young couple locked up, jumped into Paul's car and headed off.

A few hours later they were on the same road, heading in the opposite direction, with headlights seeking their way through the dark. The winter was pretty harsh that year and the first thought on both their minds as they let themselves into the cottage was to get the fire going. Breda and Paul work well as a team, so as Breda was bringing some life into the house with a blazing fire, Paul was in the kitchen whipping up some hot soup, scone bread and some piping-hot coffee. The world outside may have been fierce and cold, but Paul and Breda were safe and sound in their little cottage.

Time moved on and a few hours later the couple had almost completely forgotten about the earlier events of the day. *Top Gear*, Paul's favourite show, was just starting on the television. It wasn't exactly a firm favourite with Breda, however, so she was busy tidying up the kitchen before getting off to bed for a well-earned rest.

'WHAT?' yelled Breda, from the kitchen, over the sound of the presenter's monologue. 'Is she talking to me?' thought Paul. 'What is it Paul? Can't you manage to get up off your chair instead of calling me from there?' asked Breda as she popped her head round the kitchen corner into the room. Breda was tired and not really in the mood to act as Paul's servant. 'I didn't say anything,' replied Paul, confused at Breda's questioning. 'I'm going to bed,' was the response. 'I'm so tired I'm starting to hear things.' Breda made her way out of the living room, slamming the door in annoyance. 'Jesus,' thought Paul. 'There's no call for that carry on.'

Forty minutes later, Paul locked up the cottage, turned off the lights and made his own way to bed. Breda was fast asleep as Paul — not wanting to tempt Breda's anger — silently got undressed and settled down to sleep. As he was about to drift off, Paul heard his name being called from the middle of the room, clearly in the night air. His eyes popped open and the idea of sleep quickly disappeared. That wasn't Breda; that was a man's voice.

'Paul!' it said again, just as distinct as before. Alarmed and damn well afraid, Paul jumped out of bed and snapped on the bedside lamp. There was no one in the room. He rushed out and checked the cottage. All the doors were securely locked, as were the windows. This didn't make sense. There were only two people in the cottage: Breda and himself. Where did that voice come from?

'Breda! Wake up! Wake up!' he hissed, furiously shaking his wife out of her slumber. Breda's eyes slowly focused on her husband, who looked like a startled rabbit. 'Someone just called my name, and it was right here in the room. I've searched the house — there's no one here

A view of the peaceful village of Leighlinbridge.
© Fran McCormack, 2010.

but us.' Confused and only half awake, Breda had to get Paul to repeat himself. 'I was just about to fall asleep when I heard someone say "Paul". It wasn't my imagination as I heard it again about a minute later. What the hell …?'

'That's what I heard today,' said Breda, growing more concerned by the second. 'I heard someone call my name earlier today. Was it the same voice you heard over the phone?'

You would think two grown adults wouldn't spend the rest of the night with the light on – but Paul and Breda did. There were no more phantom name checks that night, but the couple still didn't get much sleep.

Over the next fortnight, though they heard no more, they felt very uncomfortable in what used to be their dream home. Breda refused to be home on her own, so Paul decided he'd take a few weeks' holidays from work, and try to figure out who their mystery caller was. It was easier now to make light of it all, but both Paul and Breda were very certain of what they had heard and they needed to figure it out – otherwise their

Leighlinbridge. © Fran McCormack, 2010.

dream cottage would be back on the property market pretty quickly.

Paul's first port of call was to his neighbours in the surrounding area. Wisely, though, he didn't just land up on doorsteps saying, 'I live down the road and I think our cottage is haunted. Would you know anything about it?' Instead he concocted a story of researching the history of the little cottage he and his wife had recently purchased. Being new to the area, Paul didn't really know any of his neighbours, so he didn't fancy their first impressions of him as being somewhat of a nutter.

He wasn't having much luck in his research. None of the immediate neighbours could tell Paul much about the house. These days people barely know who lives next to them, never mind a history of random little cottages, so he needed to refine his plan.

Breda still wasn't comfortable in the cottage on her own, so she waited patiently in the car as Paul did his rounds. Since the current plan of action was getting them nowhere, the couple headed back home to take stock and to see if they could figure out how to find some information on the little place they had been so happy to buy only a few short months before. The stress on a very pregnant Breda wasn't helping matters either, so the thought of selling up and moving was a real consideration. Something had to be done.

The seriousness of the situation became clear as they both sat in the kitchen in silence. 'Hello,' said a voice, this time sounding like it came from the living room. Paul and Breda looked at each other blankly, not knowing whether to run, hide or scream. Could it be possible that whatever was here was aware that the couple were trying to dig up information? Why did this voice return now, just as they had started research into the cottage? 'What in God's name do you want?' roared Paul. The silence in the cottage remained unbroken in reply.

'That's it. Let's go to the priest.'

'Priest?' said Paul. 'We haven't been to Mass in years.'

'I can't live here Paul. I want to leave.' Breda quietly started to sob.

'Right, come on; let's go to the priest then. But we both know he'll tell us it's because we don't go to Mass.'

As luck would have it, the priest wasn't home, but an excellent idea did occur to Breda as they drove along. 'I know that Mrs Kinsella lives out this way,' she said. 'Mrs Kinsella is in her eighties and has lived here most of her adult life. She might be able to tell us about the house.'

And so they visited Mrs Kinsella. 'Ah, Pat Tobert's old cottage. Pat was a lovely man, but he obviously had his demons', Mrs Kinsella said cryptically as the couple sat at her kitchen table, with two big sugary mugs of tea in front of them. 'Demons?' stammered Breda, glancing sharply at her husband. Mrs Kinsella was of the old stock – forward speaking and damn the consequences:

'The drink. He was too fond of the drink. Hanged himself in the shed outside, with a bellyful of Jameson in him. He was a terribly lonely man from what I hear, but very polite – always tipping his cap if you met him. He died sometime in the 1950s I think, some time between the forties and the fifties anyway. My memory isn't what it used to be, but I do remember he was a harmless critter. Just unfortunate in life and terribly, terribly lonely.'

After another thirty minutes of idle chat, Breda and Paul made their way back out to the car. It was crunch time. 'Breda, I think we should go back to the cottage and stay there. Let's forget about moving. If it is this fella Pat that calls our name, at least that's all he does. It would be a different story if he started appearing and scaring the bejesus out of us.' Old Pat must have been listening.

For the following three days, there were no more occurrences. Breda was starting to get used to the cottage again, so much so that Paul decided to take a trip into Carlow and get a few odds and ends sorted out. Back within the hour, his heart fell when he saw Breda sobbing at the kitchen table. What had happened? 'Why didn't she ring me?' he thought, before copping the sight of his own phone above the fridge. She didn't call because he'd left his mobile at home. 'Baby! What's wrong? Breda?' She took her head out of her hands and the look on her face was enough to give him the chills. Breda tried to speak, but instead burst out in a fresh round of sobs. All Paul could manage was a big hug, and slowly

Breda stopped crying and eventually felt ready to explain. 'I saw him Paul … I saw him in the hallway.'

'Saw who Breda? Did someone break in? Did you get a good look at him? Are you OK?' Paul was getting frantic and looking around for something heavy to use as a defence against this intruder. 'No Paul, it wasn't a person. I came in from the back yard and he was just standing in the front room doorway. He was old, he was wearing a cap … he tipped it at me and then he just vanished. He was there and then he wasn't. Am I going mad Paul?'

'No baby, no. Really, it's just your imagination.' Paul needed an answer and he needed it now. 'Before we had talked to Mrs Kinsella, your mind didn't have any visual description to latch on to. Now it does, and I suppose in an attempt to make sense of everything, you mind showed you what your brain would logically expect. It's OK, really.' Paul's explanation calmed his already fragile wife. 'No matter what, I have to get her out of here,' thought Paul. 'This stress can't be good for the baby.'

'I'll tell you what we'll do,' suggested Paul. 'I'll take you to your mother's and you can stay there for a few days. In the meantime – just so you know there's nothing haunting this place – I'll stay here. I guarantee that within a few days, everything will be back to normal.'

On his way back from Breda's mother's house, where he had left his wife with the excuse that Breda found the cottage to be too far from town in her present condition, Paul mulled over the recent events in his head. He didn't for one minute believe his own explanation. He needed advice about ghosts and he needed it now.

The internet is an amazing place and Paul was stunned to find plenty of internet forums dedicated to just this kind of thing. Who would have ever thought? 'But then, the internet itself is almost paranormal,' he thought, 'it exists, it interacts, but you can't see it.' Settled in the front room with his MacBook, Paul searched for a few minutes, found an Irish forum and quickly registered. It was the paranormal forum on Boards.ie, so it didn't take long for Paul to receive replies to his cryptic post, which asked 'What can you do to get rid of a ghost?'

'Go see a doctor' was one reply. 'Stop taking drugs' was another. Eventually the cynicism changed to requests for more information, which Paul couldn't bring himself to supply, what with the whole 'first impressions' idea and sounding like a nutter, but one reply caught his attention, 'If you experience paranormal activity in your home and it disturbs you, loudly tell the spirit you now own the house, and tell them you want to them to leave. That's what Ghost Hunters say you should do.' Why hadn't he thought of that himself? It made perfect sense. However, the poster didn't explain just *when* Paul should do this. Should he wait for another paranormal occurrence, when he could be certain the ghost was actually there and listening? Or do ghosts hear everything anyway?

Paul sat in the kitchen and tried his damnedest to contact Pat. He yelled his name, asked him to 'make himself known'.

The Black Castle. © Fran McCormack, 2010.

Nothing. Not a sausage. He'd been at this for two full hours and all he had heard so far was a cat out in the yard. 'Maybe this is nonsense,' he thought, 'or maybe we are both going mad.' Such things can happen. Maybe there's some kind of weird radiation in the house; maybe that's what caused Pat to kill himself in the first place. Making a mental note to look these up theories like this one on the web, Paul put on the kettle and turned to watch a bit of telly before bed.

He froze solid when he heard his name being called from the living room. Then, when the figure of an old man popped out of nowhere in the living room doorway, Paul thought he was ready to faint. He didn't though. Instead he started yelling at the top of his voice, 'Please leave us alone. This is our house and you are scaring my wife! Please go! Wave goodbye if you intend to leave now!' He tactically left out admitting that he was absolutely terrified himself. Still, to his amazement, not only did the apparition tip his cap at Paul, he also mouthed the word 'Sorry' and waved goodbye. As suddenly as he had appeared, he vanished.

One of Ireland's earliest Norman castles, the Black Castle, was built to protect the river crossing. © Fran McCormack, 2010.

Now Paul fainted.

Birds were singing when Paul awoke, sprawled on the kitchen floor. Did he dream all that? If he did, why wasn't he in a warm bed, instead of on a cold floor? The place did feel different though – not that it felt bad to begin with, but now it just felt happier, safer. Breda returned to her dream home a few days later and it took Paul upwards of two years to tell her the full story. He only felt right telling her once he was certain that Pat had indeed moved on. Plus he felt awfully stupid recounting his experience because, really, it was a tad mad.

Ghosts? He certainly wouldn't believe in them, except for the fact he saw one, as did Breda. As the years passed, the couple not only raised a healthy family, but after a few years of living in the cottage, ghost free, they made it a point to pour themselves a small glass of Jameson, once a year, in memory of old Mr Tobert. He was indeed, as Mrs Kinsella had said, a 'harmless critter' ... and he also kept his word.

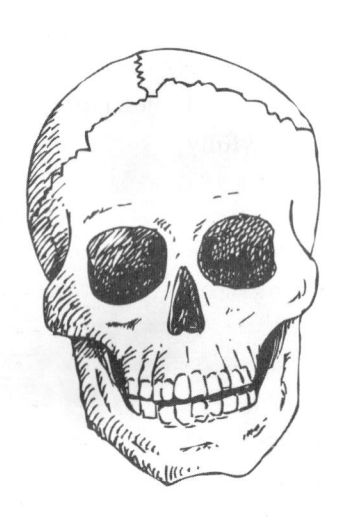

6

Brown Street Ghost Story

ONE of the everlasting effects of researching this book is that it's hard to look at Carlow Town in the same light as before. Streets that had never before even suggested the idea of a haunting now take on new significance. Such an effect is bolstered when the account has never before been published and comes straight from the proverbial horse's mouth.

In the middle of the town, linking Dublin Street to College Street, is a small, old and narrow passageway called Brown Street. It's here that our next story takes place, as sent in to us by a Carlow resident. We won't give away the exact address on Brown Street, nor the name of our correspondent, but you can be assured it is as authentic as they come.

So now, let us pass the candle to our Brown Street ghost witness and let them take us through the events first hand:

'The events in this story took place in Brown Street, right in the centre of town. That place was always busy, what with seven of us students living there, but when the Easter holidays came along and everyone else went home I decided to stay on, liking my own company and a bit of peace and quiet. I should tell you now that it was a three-storey terraced house, and that next door was derelict. The lads told me about a student who'd hanged himself in that house and that the rafters were still visible where he'd torn away the plaster to expose the beams. One day we managed to get in over the wall and through a window, and sure enough, in one of the rooms on the second floor there was a section of ceiling about a foot square where the beams were exposed. It was odd though, that there were no stairs to be found to the third floor and my attempt to go up there is another story altogether.

Anyway, the first night I was in the house by myself I was in my room on the third floor listening to music when I began to hear thumping sounds. I wasn't sure what was causing them, so I went back downstairs, turning on all the lights as I went, because I thought it must

Carlow is a well-known student town.
© Fran McCormack, 2010.

be one or more of the lads come back, home having done their head or heads in. No. Nothing. Not thinking much of it, I went back up the stairs to my room. As soon as I got settled on the bed with my book I could hear it again. Only this time the thumping seemed a little more regular; it sounded like someone on the stairs. I couldn't tell whether they were going up or down but I knew there was no one next door, which was where my room backed onto. I got up again, only this time I didn't go downstairs, I just hollered the names of my housemates from the landing on the top floor. No one answered. It was late enough so I decided to go to sleep; it must just be an old house creaking. Either that, or something was going on somewhere of which I was unaware.

Daylight came and the house was just as it always was when everyone was there, only quiet, no stereos or shouts from one floor to another. I was a voracious reader and was delighted to get the chance to read novels at one sitting (or lying down, I should say, which was much more comfortable).

Night came again and so did the noises. This time they were more distinct; someone was going up and down the stairs and doors were opening and closing at the hand of someone who shouldn't be there. Now I was scared. It was enough that I could hear the footsteps running closer to me, but with the doors going as well I didn't know when my bedroom door would fly open. So I grabbed the flashlight and made my way to John's room where I knew there was a Japanese short sword. I'd watched enough crime dramas to know how to hold a flashlight and weapon pointed forward to sweep every room on each floor of the house. I worked my way down, looking for trouble, and found nothing. I brought the sword to bed with me that night.

Next day I moved whatever food I had in the house up to my room, along with the milk and kettle. I'd had the mickey taken out of me by Dave for buying powdered milk ("… with all the cows in the country?") but I was glad I did. There was no way I was going downstairs again later that night. I made sure, as I always did, that the front and back doors were locked and every window was closed. Every internal door was closed too.

It was worse than before. Doors didn't just open and close – they slammed. Footsteps on the stairs were at a running pace, thumping heavily on every board, and there was I with the flashlight beside me, saving the batteries, getting up occasionally to face the door with the sword

The college, Carlow. © Fran McCormack, 2010.

Brown Street – scene of poltergeist activity.
© Fran McCormac, 2010.

Another view of Brown Street © Fran McCormack, 2010.

in my hand. After a couple of hours I couldn't take anymore, so I hopped up and ran to the landing, and I know it's a cliché, but the air turned blue for the next ten minutes or so. I cursed whatever was making those noises, swore that I didn't care if it was in hell or purgatory or somewhere else but that I wasn't budging and that if it hadn't been to hell then it could go there for all I cared. In fact, I was wishing it there because I was not leaving. And it stopped.

I wasn't troubled by anything like what I'd experienced over those few nights but that wasn't the end of it. The last occurred on a bright day in May, near the end of that academic year. I was seated on the windowsill by the third-floor landing, smoking a rollie and soaking up the sun. I leaned out of the window to catch the light and I noticed someone walking from one room to the other. Now, when I say someone, I mean that I saw the lowest part of someone – a pair of black Doc boots and faded-to-grey jeans – walk into Stevo and James's room. That's all I saw. No one could have got past me, for if you take the landing as a narrow cruciform, the window was to the left, the stairs behind me, the lads' room to the right, and me and Robbie's room to the top. There was no other exit past me. I knew Robbie was away and called out the others' names. No response. I pushed their door open, looked in and saw no one.

I know there's some would say I'm an awful liar, but I tell you this, I'm glad I'm in a new house, in a new estate and not looking at something that I can't see but can feel, just by the hairs prickling my arm or the temperature falling beside me.'

Remember that story as you walk up Brown Street in the dead of night and just hope there are no ghostly eyes watching you from an upper window.

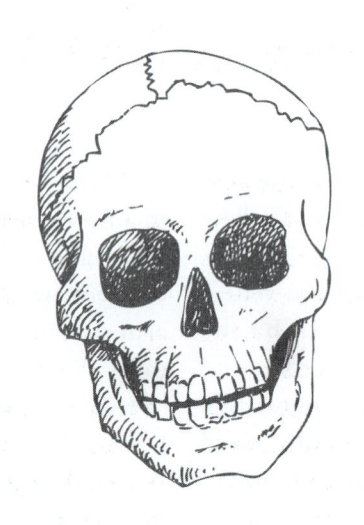

7
A Paranormal Investigation

As we have already mentioned, there is more to the old Carlow Gaol than meets the eye. After the gaol closed down, the premises were taken over by Thomas Thompson, who started business as a mechanical engineer in 1878. Still in business today, and still in Carlow, Thompson's manufactured Ireland's first suspension bridge in 1906, plus, amongst many other things, wings and struts for Bristol fighter planes during the First World War. We have talked to people who worked in Thompson's during the 1950s and '60s, many of whom have commented on the apparent reports of a child ghost, as well as the sound of a heavy door slamming – usually referred to as some kind of phantom cell door being slammed shut on some poor unfortunate.

We'll come back to reports from the era when the site was owned by Thompson's a little later, but the apparent haunting by a young child and the slamming door sound both became a talking point in early 2009, when KCLR aired their live FrightNight from the shopping centre.

The station brought thirteen people, as well as two representatives from Leinster Paranormal, to the shopping centre for what was initially probably just a marketing stunt; bring people to an apparently haunted place, switch off the lights and let human nature and its 'fight or flight' response take it from there. This group of people, though, probably got more than they bargained for.

Paranormal investigators sometimes use what is called an 'EMF' detector, which is basically a device electricians use to detect electro-magnetic frequencies. These frequencies can be natural or created by manmade electrical devices. If these frequencies are too high in an area, they can affect people in some pretty strange ways. People susceptible to EMF can feel as though someone is watching them, they can feel paranoid and even nauseous. These symptoms can also match apparent paranormal activity, which is why EMF detectors are used in investigations; a lot of the time the cause isn't a ghost but a naturally high level of EMF, especially if the radiation is detected

What was the cause of the door slams and sounds heard by the KCLR FrightNight team in Carlow Shopping Centre? © Fran McCormack, 2010.

in the same place all the time. When you turn off the electrical device, the electromagnetic field will essentially disappear, as the source of the field would have been switched off, but, essentially, EMF won't move from the device that is emitting it, unless you move the device. If it's natural and coming from the ground, it will be there all the time, regardless.

Leinster Paranormal conducted thorough EMF sweeps throughout the shopping centre and found some peculiar oddities in one area. One upstairs part of the centre had no electricity, which means there would was no manmade sources of EMF in that particular area. But that didn't stop the team's detectors going off randomly. Electromagnetic fields were detected floating throughout the upstairs area, which lacked the power supply to create such fields. As well as that, these EM fields were wandering about the place — here one minute, over there the next — and periodically they weren't to be found anywhere for prolonged stretched of time. Maybe an electrician would like to contact us and put us straight, but electromagnetic radiation isn't meant to work like that. (In fact, if you are an authority on electromagnetic fields and how they function and can explain that for us, please look at the back of the book for contact details and get in touch.)

The other side to the paranormal's relation to electromagnetic fields is that 'apparently' (and I think that deserves inverted commas) ghosts manipulate the electromagnetic field, which can therefore be detected by an EMF meter. It's a hard theory to validate, as normally one would assume that any EM field would be natural (unless there was no power source at all in the area), and since EM fields can affect our brains — which essentially are also electromagnetic — then EMF meters don't really detect ghosts. Still though, considering the lack of any power source near enough for the EMF meters to pick up radiation, just where were those EM fields coming from that were being detected? Hold that thought, as we'll be coming back to this same area of the centre pretty soon. Let's get back to our story.

The KCLR crew, the thirteen 'lucky' guests and the Leinster Paranormal reps were at this stage locked in the centre, as the centre manager had locked up and left about ten minutes previously. It didn't take long for things to start happening, as Iris, one of the KCLR crew, soon found out:

'Myself, Steven and Norma have come into the changing area here. We were completely alone and very, very clearly we heard a loud slam — like a heavy, metal door slamming. There's no door like that anywhere near us, plus we've been hearing other noises which are definitely coming from the middle of the centre. It is extremely eerie in here, but we definitely and very clearly heard a loud door slamming and other noises.'

At this time, everyone was in the same upstairs area, which had no power — all on the same floor. No one else, though, had heard the slamming door or any noises coming from the main centre area.

Upstairs in Carlow Shopping Centre, where the FrightNight team based themselves. © Fran McCormack, 2010.

The next logical step, therefore, was to bring everyone into the room in which Iris, Steve and Norma had heard the slamming noise. Another paranormal investigation technique was used, in which one of the EMF devices, a particular model with five different coloured lights on it called a 'K2' was used as a 'trigger device'. There was a green light for the on/off state, plus green, yellow, orange and red lights indicating the different levels of signal strength. The plan was very simple: try to communicate with the 'spirit' and see if it could light up the colour of light asked for. (You can actually hear what happened next by visiting http://www.radiocrackle.com/radio/KCLRs_FrightNight.mp3)

For those reading this in a normal, honest-to-goodness book made of pages (rather than a digital format), let me explain what happens. Everyone, as already mentioned, is in the same upstairs room conducting a 'trigger device' experiment, when, from outside the room, in the main part of the shopping centre, comes the oft reported slamming door sound. It's very clear, it's very loud and it certainly wasn't made by any of the people who were there. It's important to remember the shopping centre itself was locked from the outside, with the only inhabitants all in that small upstairs room.

Amidst the ensuing pandemonium, one of the Leinster Paranormal team and a KCLR presenter went around all the doors within the centre, live on the radio, trying to recreate what had just been heard, but to no avail. Virtually all the doors that could be opened or closed were spring mounted and as a result, couldn't really be slammed – even if there was someone there to slam one.

Could this be the same sound Dominic hears virtually everyday outside his office, as described in a previous chapter? Where does it come from? Is this the same slamming door sound workers from Thompson's also reported hearing all those years ago? Could it really be a phantom cell door?

For now, all that can be said is that there was indeed the sound of a heavy door slamming, but it could not be replicated. Plus, who would have slammed it anyway? Everyone at that stage was in the same room and the sound itself most definitely did not come from outside the centre (as is clear to hear on the KCLR recording).

In their various visits to Carlow Gaol, Leinster Paranormal have reported hearing that same sound on more than one occasion, but to date have not managed to track down its source. They also have never managed to explain the moving EM fields which seem to be most common in the one area of the gaol/shopping centre that has no power.

If that wasn't enough, KCLR presenter Steven literally had a 'fright night' and a memory he'll never forget. As the night progressed, the group was split in two. Steven's group was in this same, unpowered part of the centre and were in the process of what can be referred to as 'calling out'. Basically, to 'call out' is to chill out and chew the fat with any apparent 'ghosts' in the hope they respond. People normally explain why they are there, that they mean no harm and that they are just curious, and ask if the spirit could let them know in any way that they are there. It's just another experiment in the paranormal researcher's armoury. You don't necessarily have to believe that spirits exist, but if they do and you don't try to directly communicate with them, then you aren't really doing the job properly. It was during one of these sessions that Steven had quite a startling experience:

'I'm convinced I saw the shape of a small person sitting in the little room opposite me. I looked a number of times, doing as Leinster Paranormal had suggested in their prep talk (if you think you see something, look away, refresh your vision and look back). I did this numerous times, but the figure was still there. I told the others, and started towards the door of the room.'

Cue more of the strange EMF readings. Throughout the whole session, the K2 device hadn't even flickered. As the

KCLR, LeinsterParanormal and guests took part in a paranormal investigation in Carlow Shopping Centre.
© Fran McCormack, 2010.

group moved to where Steven had seen the small figure, the meter started going crazy, then stopped, then started again before randomly moving around. Finally, it stayed in one spot and another trigger object experiment started. Since Steven thought he had seen a small child, the focus was on that – 'light red if you are a girl, green if you are a boy', etc. – and by the time the group had finished they were quite convinced they'd been communicating with the ghost of a small girl. They had no idea that this same ghost of a female child had been reported in Thompson's many years before.

So, what do we have so far? Slamming doors, ghostly kids, friendly poltergeists? How about some mysterious lights?

Within that one public investigation, numerous mysterious lights were seen. In the cellar of Cafe le Monde (which had been the Governor's House), both groups independently reported seeing moving lights in the darkness. The cellar area is quite small and any light getting into that area can be easily identified, but both groups reported trails of light moving across the walls. These couldn't be replicated, though various attempts were made on the night. Similarly, it wasn't a case of one group influencing the other, as neither group knew the other had had the same experience until later. All in all a pretty strange set of experiences and one which will probably never be fully explained.

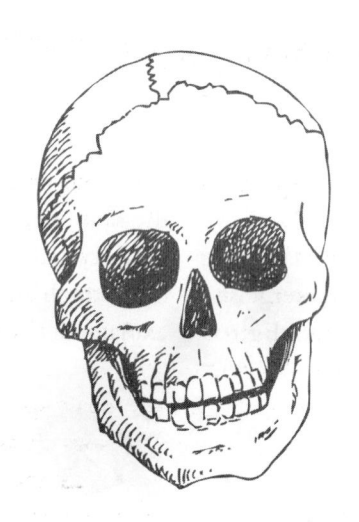

8

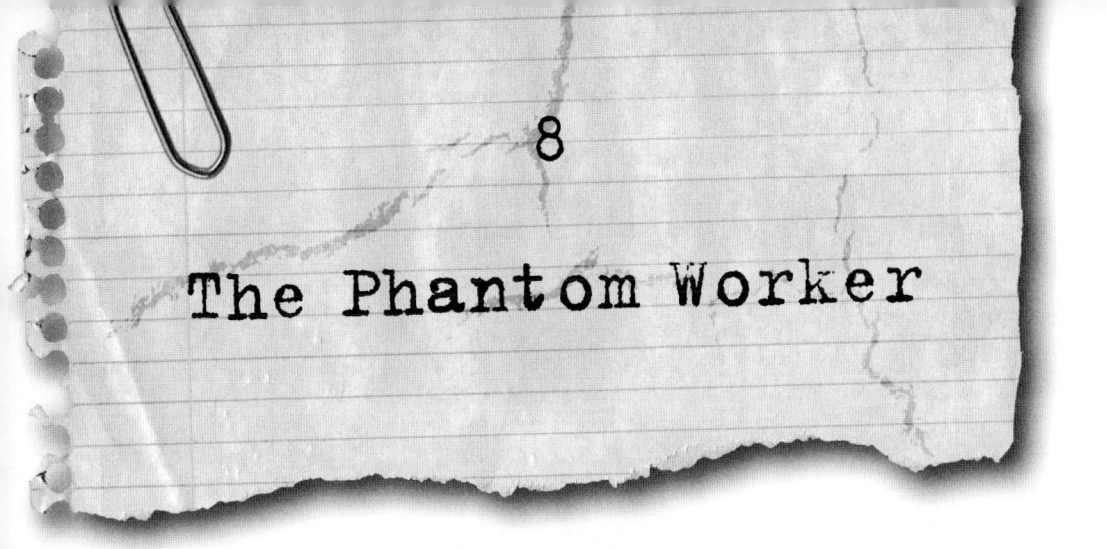

The Phantom Worker

BEFORE we move on from Carlow Shopping Centre/Gaol, there is one more story. This time we'll go back to the mid-1980s, when Thompson's were manufacturing truck bodies. We recently had a quick chat with an ex-Thompson's employee who used to spray the truck bodies:

'Back around 1983 or 1984 I was working in Thompson's as a sprayer. My job was to spray the truck bodies. During one work day, my manager asked if I would leave early and come back later that night, as there was a job coming within the following few hours and it would need to be sprayed and finished up that night. "No problem," I said, not for one minute having any reservations about working on my own. If he had asked me to do the same thing the following morning, he might well have got a difference answer.

I arrived back at work at 7 p.m. that evening, met my manager, and spent some time discussing the aspects of the job at hand. At the time, Thompson's was divided into different workspaces, so after the manager had left, I didn't really know if there were any other workers in the premises. It didn't matter to me anyway. Although I'd heard the odd story here and there about the place, I assumed any ghost stories were idle gossip. Besides, I'm not easily spooked.

It was almost 8 p.m. by the time I had my equipment set up and was ready to start spraying. Almost as soon as I started the compressor and started spraying, I could hear hammering from elsewhere in the workshop – heavy hammering on steel as well as the sound of heavy steel slamming on the ground. I didn't think anything of it to be honest, I just kept on working. What piqued my interest though, after a while, was that although I could hear these sounds while I worked, any time I stopped, the place was quiet.

The hours flew by until it came time to have a break and grab a bite to eat. I have to say I was absolutely convinced at this stage that there were others working nearby, due to the loud sounds I'd been hearing, so when I got to the canteen, I expected to meet the other workers, who

61

Hanover Works as it was when owned by Thompson's.
© Fran McCormack, 2010.

would have been taking a break at the same time. I switched off the compressor, grabbed my lunchbox and, convinced the other workers were on a break as the place was once again silent, I made my way up to the canteen. It was completely deserted.

You have to understand that even at this stage I didn't think anything was amiss. I assumed whoever had been working had finished up and left, though the thought did strike me that I should have heard their exit, considering how noisy the main doors were. Still, I thought no more of it and ate my lunch. After I'd finished eating, I decided to stretch my legs a bit and talk a walk around, since I had only used up about half of my break time. I always enjoyed exploring the building. Unlike now, much of the original gaol was still in existence. The old cells were still there, with their heavy steel doors in durable steel frames. Many of the cells were used as storage, with contents dating back to before the First World War, when Thompson's used to make parts for Bristol planes. As I walked around, I kept an eye out for other workers, which, looking back, makes me realise I was actually a bit more freaked out about the sounds than I thought I was at the time.

I met no one on my walk about and the whole workshop was very quiet, so when I got back to my workspace, I was satisfied that I was on my own. Imagine my surprise, then – and horror, it has to be said – when no sooner had I started to work, than I heard those same hammering noises again. I had to reason this out, and came to the conclusion that my compressor unit must be acting up, or I was hearing noises from outside that one mightn't hear during the day, when the workshop was busy. I knuckled down to work once again but within ten minutes those same hammering noises began again, this time accompanied by the odd loud slam of steel on concrete. There was no way these sounds were coming from outside, and, since was certain I was on my own, there was also no way these sounds were coming from the inside of the building. There was only one thing to do, and that was to go walkabout and see if I could solve this puzzle once and for all.

Off I went. I don't know if I was eventually beginning to get freaked out a bit or what, but the atmosphere had changed. Even though I knew I was the only person here, it still felt as though I wasn't on my own. Maybe I had missed the other worker on my last walk around the workshop. They may have been in the bathroom, or maybe we could have bypassed each other (which, considering the layout, was a possibility). Maybe that could explain why I not only felt I wasn't on my own, but why I was increasingly getting the impression that I was being watched as I made my way through the building.

After another fifteen minutes searching, it got to the stage where I just had to get back to work. It was early morning and I had a job to get finished. I had looked everywhere I could. I'd even been calling out "hello" as loud as seemed reasonable every now and then, but I had neither got a reply nor seen any sign of life. Though it didn't ease the feeling of being watched, I made my way back to my workspace. I hadn't much left to do at this stage; it was just a matter of finishing up a few bits and tidying away my equipment, so I restarted the compressor with gusto and was fully focused on the task at hand. I started working and things went well; for the next thirty minutes or so I was engrossed in finishing up the paint job. I had completely forgotten about the sounds and the eerie feeling of being watched, right up until the hammering started up again – loud this time and for some reason sounding much closer than it had previously. There were more sounds this time; instead of one person working, it sounded like a small army were making a tank somewhere on the premises. Startled, I looked up. I have no idea why I looked at the spot I focused on, but being on top of the truck body let me see over to the very far end of the building. There was someone standing there. It's a hard thing to describe, as people may ask why I didn't jump up and run out of there, but I was rooted to the spot. I was looking at a person at the far end of the building, yet this sound of furious steel working, hammering and slamming was coming from the other side of the building, closer to me, so whoever I was looking at wasn't the person working. There were obviously at least two other people here, yet twice I could find no one. This was the one time that the sounds kept going after I switched off the compressor, which I did in a hurry, convinced someone was trying to rob the place. The sounds didn't seem to matter to me at this stage, as my brain was more concerned with the identity of the person I had seen. The sounds were of someone working, so if someone had broken in just to do some work, then fine, but the person on the other side of the building was staring straight at me. Whoever this person was, they'd obviously been there a while, which was why I'd felt like someone was watching me, so I made sure the exit doors were secure and I went off in pursuit.

It was a good ten minutes later, after I had searched the area thoroughly, that I realised the hammering had stopped. I shouted out, ran to the exit doors to check no one had left and found them still securely locked from the inside. Then, still convinced that what I had seen was a real, living person, and intrigued by who the mysterious worker that had been hammering metal and steel all night was, I went searching again. I shouted, I called out, I ran around, getting from A to B as quickly as I could to ensure I didn't accidentally run past the people I was searching for – but I found no one.

I had finished my work but I was confused. The main doors were still locked securely. In my head, things were pretty muddled. I *had* seen someone and I had definitely heard the sounds I had heard, yet there was no one here but me. The only logical conclusion I could come to was that the person I had seen, and the second person who had obviously been working, had both left by some other exit, though I couldn't fathom which exit. Still, it was very early in the morning. I was getting tired and thought that the sense of dread I was feeling must surely be down to the tiredness and not because I flat out could not explain my experiences so far that night. The best thing I could do, I thought, was pack away my gear and go home.

I went back to my workspace and started tidying up my equipment. This isn't something all workers would do, but cleaning and looking after the equipment meant it worked properly when I needed it to, so it was a habit I had formed over the years. "Bam! Slam! Crash!" I couldn't believe it. Within five minutes of abandoning my search the noises had started again – this time much, much louder. In fact, they sounded like they were coming from the workspace right beside mine. "Ah ha!" I thought. "Whoever is making those sounds definitely won't have the time to hide themselves this time," and with that in mind I rushed around to the next workspace. Empty. But I could still clearly hear the hammering. I checked the next one, the following workspace, and the one after that. All empty. Why, then, was the hammering sound still apparently emanating from the workspace beside my own? How was that possible when I was only after checking it?

I rechecked the areas I had just checked and still nothing. When I entered the suspected workspace, the one beside my

On the factory floor of Thompson's. Courtesy of Thompson's, Carlow.

own, the place unexpectedly fell quiet. Not only that but it really, really felt like someone was standing right behind me staring at my neck. I suppose I could have stayed there, rooted to the spot, but instinctively I spun round, found there was no one there and decided that enough was enough. I'd clean the equipment tomorrow – right now I was getting out of there. Fast.

I rushed in to my work area, grabbed my coat and lunch container, unlocked the door and almost ran through another worker who was just about to knock on the door to begin the early shift. I couldn't believe it; it was 5 a.m. I had spent hours in there after finishing the spray job and I didn't realise it. I have no idea what the other guy thought, but I ran past him with barely a glance and didn't stop running until I reached my car. I got into the car and tried to get my head around what had happened. There was no one in that building but me all night, yet I had seen someone and I had heard someone hammering and working metal. How was that possible?

Thompson's made parts for First World War aeroplanes in the Carlow plant. Courtesy of Thompson's, Carlow.

Before this, I had only heard the odd snippet of stories about the old gaol being haunted. When I went to work the following day, I wasn't too sure if I should mention this to anyone at all. They'd think I was mad. The manager was happy with the work I'd done, and when he came to talk to me I asked if there was anyone else scheduled to work last night. "No one", he said. That was part of the reason he had been there to meet me, to ensure I got into the building in the first place, since it would normally be locked up at that time of night. My manager sensed my confusion and he needled me to explain why I would have got any other impression.

"What the heck," I thought. I knew I'd sound like a fool, but I told him the whole story. I told him of the noises, I told him of what I had assumed was an intruder, I told him about my searches – everything. I wrapped it all up by explaining that I had no idea what to make of it, that I wasn't going mad and that I'd still work at night whenever he needed me to regardless. I fully expected to become that day's laughing stock, but instead my manager gave me a knowing smile and said, "Ah, so we can add you to the list then as well."

As I mentioned before, I had heard the odd, vague rumour about hauntings in the Gaol, but nothing too specific and never from a first-hand witness. That changed, though, as word of my experiences spread to other workers who had experienced almost exactly the same things in virtually the same scenario. I never experienced it again though. I don't know if I'd like to, because now I know for sure that I was in the place on my own, whereas at the time I was convinced there were other people there, but at least I know I wasn't imagining it. When I got home in the dawn of that morning, I was seriously beginning to doubt my own sanity. The idea that I'd just had a paranormal experience was too farfetched to consider. At least now I know it's the other way around; I wasn't going mad and I actually did have a brief encounter with the paranormal.'

That was a word-for-word account, straight from the horse's mouth, about his experience working in Thompson's in the early 1980s. There are some intriguing similarities there, specifically that loud slamming noise. What's also interesting is the description of the old cell doors. Though long gone, could they be the origin of the loud, metallic sounds heard by Cafe le Monde staff and by the KCLR crew on their FrightNight? Who knows, but next time you're in Carlow Shopping Centre, keep your wits about you. Of the many people who visit the centre everyday, there's a chance at least one of them may not actually be living.

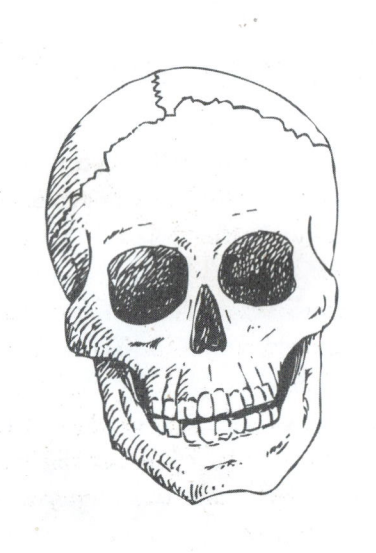

9

The Students and the Poltergeist

CARLOW is well known as a student town, a history some would say can be traced back to 1782, when St Patrick's Seminary first opened. Granted, it was a seminary rather than a college *per se*, but you get the idea.

There is one big problem when it comes to ghost stories and students; being migrational beings, students tend to be from outside the county, and when they leave, so too do accounts of their paranormal experiences in the town. The end result is that it's pretty hard to track down student accounts of any paranormal experiences.

We've already brought you one student account of a paranormal disturbance in Brown Street and we now have a second poltergeist account from a student. It's worth noting that many people explain poltergeist activity with mental duress or stress. When you consider the pressure students can be under at exam time, maybe it isn't too surprising to find that they have a tendency to report poltergeist-like experiences. Alternatively, maybe poltergeists enjoy the student lifestyle – who knows?

Part of our research process was to set up a Twitter account and a Facebook page, encouraging people to get in touch and share their experiences with us. Many did, and this was one of the more chillingly interesting accounts. Our source asked to remain anonymous, but we can tell you our source is male and this encounter took place in Carlow just after the turn of the twenty-first century:

'In the early autumn of 2001, I was flat hunting in Carlow. I was a student from Wicklow, in my second year of a three-year course at college in Carlow. I teamed up with a fellow student in the quest to find the perfect accommodation and it wasn't too long before we found a two-storey house on a housing estate. Retrospect is a fine thing; the only problem with it is you don't see it until after the fact, but really, from day one we should have noticed the issues that I personally only realised after years of reflection.

It's about time, I suppose, I introduced you to Jimmy. He was what one would

St Patrick's Seminary, Carlow. © Fran McCormack, 2010.

class as a trendy student – I think at this stage he was trying to be a goth. He called himself goth, as the 1980s were making a comeback, but we just classed him as "emo" to wind him up a bit. Overall though, Jimmy was a very nice chap; humorous, intelligent and always the one with the answers. It was Jimmy who I had teamed up with in search for somewhere to live, so it was the pair of us who now found ourselves at this house, about to meet our prospective landlord and view the premises.

The house looked lovely. It was a nice estate, although admittedly there weren't many student rentals there. The rent was refreshingly cheap (another signal?) and the owner showed us through a busy family home. Supper had obviously just finished, as the husband and wife were in the throes of washing up and the two kids were in their rooms doing homework. We duly followed our soon-to-be landlord throughout the building as he showed us the rooms, explained how the heating worked and basically gave us the royal tour, as if we weren't two down-and-out, shabbily dressed students (never mind the fact that Jimmy had make-up on!).

All we cared about at this stage was that there was a good chance the landlord would rent to us and that it would be startlingly cheap – much better than we could ever have imagined. We didn't ask ourselves just why it was so cheap, and we didn't even begin to wonder why someone would want to rent out a family home to a couple of students who looked like characters from *The Young Ones*. I got adventurous. "Are you leaving Carlow?" I asked. I really didn't care, but the man was being so nice and respectful to us, I thought I'd at least feign some interest. "Not really leaving, as such," he explained. "I work in the town, but I have another house just outside Portlaoise, so we'll be moving there." Part of me did think that didn't make sense, but that thought was quickly quashed by the part of my mind that didn't want to lose out on a good deal. And so the dreaded deal was struck that very day – a Friday. We could move in on the Monday, which was another aspect I'd be wondering about a few years later, when it had all eventually settled in my mind. Those people were obviously quite anxious to move to Portlaoise.

The rent was so affordable that we could actually manage to pay the first term's payment and so we pre-paid for October, November and December of that year. With just a bit of imagination, the three-bedroom house could have four bedrooms, so we moved the furniture from the front room into the living area of the kitchen and replaced it with a bed. Then we were joined by Jimmy's girlfriend, a fellow student called Ciaran and a brickie from England called Ron. Ron had been lured to Ireland by the outrageous wage packets builders were managing to bring in. He was saving it though, so cheap accommodation was right up his street. But we soon learned that there is a limit to what one is prepared to endure for the sake of cheap accommodation.

The first few weeks in the house were comfortable. We were all taking a bit of time to get used to each other, the house and our neighbours. There were no major issues except for Ciaran complaining that his room was cold. The heating was fine in the house and no one else had any problems with the heat, so I chalked Ciaran down as a bit of complainer.

As it happened, my girlfriend at the time, Sarah, lived in the adjoining housing estate. Periodically she'd drop by while out walking her dog and it was on one of these visits that we accidentally discovered another issue with Ciaran's room. Sarah had been talking to Ciaran about his cold room, who was in the midst of complaining about it again. I'd honestly never gone into his room to check if it was cold or not, but it was the first thing Sarah suggested. Before I could put her off the idea, she was gone.

I was still downstairs with the dog, Bananas, when I heard her shout, "Come up here, quick!" I made my way upstairs with the dog to find out what the commotion was about. "Seriously," Sarah was saying, "it's freezing in here." I went in to feel for myself and Bananas – obviously not one for the cold – made a frantic leap out of my arms and escaped to the landing, where he sat down, patiently looking over at me. I could swear he was trying to mentally send me the message, "I wouldn't go in there if I were you." Maybe he was.

The room was indeed absolutely and completely freezing. It was one of the weirdest experiences I had had up until then. The landing was warm, the doorway was warmish, but once you got to the centre of the room, it was damned cold. From the hallway, Bananas started up some frenzied barking, then whimpering, before moving to the good old tried and tested fierce growling. If anything grabs the attention of a human, it's a tiny little dog, hairs upright, fiercely growling at nothing. My first thought was that we must have rats and that that was why the place was so cheap. I picked Bananas up and tried to bring him back into the room, but he was having none of it and he was in mid-air by the time I crossed the threshold. I picked him up again and this time I held tight. I got into the room – dog scrambling frantically – and the second his paws touched the ground, he tore back out to the safety of the landing. It may sound cruel, but this process was repeated about ten times. I was fascinated. This dog didn't like this cold room one tiny bit. What was the story here?

I don't think the word "paranormal" crossed my mind; not until Sarah half jokingly suggested the place was haunted. Even when it did cross my mind, it didn't linger. Haunted indeed. Ghosts were more impossible than my passing my course with flying colours, which, let's be honest, was pretty impossible. "Haven't you ever heard of cold spots?" she asked. "Or that animals can sense ghosts?" Ciaran backed up my point of view. "Sarah," he said, "no matter what way you look at it, a cold room doesn't mean the paranormal. Ghosts? Really? I would never have guessed you were part of the gullible brigade. All that ghost stuff is rubbish. Gullible people who like getting ripped off by 'psychics' is what that's all about." I readily agreed. We'd been in the place for almost a month so we would know about any ghosts by now surely (if they existed, that is). One cold room and a freaked out dog a haunting does not make. I've often wondered afterwards if whatever was in the house decided then and there that it would teach us a lesson in the weeks that followed.

At this stage I should describe the layout of the rooms in the house – pay attention to this, as it'll make it much easier later to get an idea of where everyone was in relation to each other. When you enter the front of the house, you are in small hallway. Directly on the left is the door to Ron's room and directly on the right is the stairway to the upper floor. The only other door downstairs is the one directly in front at the far end of the small hallway. This door leads into the kitchen/living area, which is basically a small, open-plan kitchen that has a little living area with sofa and chairs. Downstairs, therefore, is basically made up of Ron's room and the kitchen/living area. Directly above the front door and hallway, and partially over Ron's room, was a bedroom. Adjacent to that was the master bedroom – Ciaran's room – which was directly above the kitchen and above part of Ron's room. Beside Ciaran's room was the final bedroom in the house, and beside it (at the top of the stairs) was the bathroom.

So, now it's time to introduce you to Ron, our labourer from the UK. Ron normally kept to himself, but as the weeks went by, I got to know Ron pretty well. On one particularly warm afternoon, Ciaran was upstairs studying hard and Ron and I were talking quietly in Ron's room. The door was wide open to the hallway outside, giving us a perfect view of the stairs. All was normal. Ciaran came down the stairs and offered us a coffee. We declined but he made one for himself and carried it upstairs. As I say, everything was quite normal, so it was a bit of a shock to hear a roar of anger from Ciaran, then the sound of his mug hitting the ground. Tearing back down the stairs, Ciaran was fury animated.

"What the hell are you playing at? Why did you do that? Why?" Ciaran roared at us both. I was stunned, "We haven't moved from here Ciaran – what's wrong?" But before I'd finished my sentence, Ciaran was making his way, in a run, back up the stairs, "So you're telling me neither of you did this?" he roared from the upstairs landing.

I ran up the stairs and it was immediately obvious something was very much amiss. Strewn everywhere were remnants of the contents of Ciaran's room, as if it has exploded. On the carpet in the hallway directly outside his door, and on the stairs below, were pens, markers, pieces of Ciaran's technical equipment, bits of solder, coins, knick knacks – literally every small object that had been in the room.

Two things were going on here: my eyes were looking at a scene of devastation, and my brain had concluded we had rented a room to a complete and utter nutjob. There's no way this could have happened without us hearing it downstairs. The bed was reduced to its separate components and scattered throughout the room. Ciaran's large heavy study desk was wedged securely between the tall wardrobe and a portable TV, which itself was wedged against the ceiling. Clothes were everywhere, including a shirt tied to the light fixture. But we had been right downstairs and we hadn't heard a thing, so that meant that not only was Ciaran insane enough to wreck the place and then accuse us, but he obviously dedicated himself to wrecking the room in complete silence. How insane would that make him?

While I was thinking all this, Ciaran was cursing us up and down and roaring uncontrollably. I looked him in the face and said, "Ciaran, I've no idea what's going on here, but this has nothing to do with us. It's impossible to do this kind of damage, in silence in less than the five minutes it took to you to make the cup of coffee." I went back downstairs, trying to figure out how we could get rid of this loopy individual without paying back his deposit. By this time Ciaran had turned on Ron. It wasn't until later that I thought that Ciaran was more than likely having the same thoughts about us. In any event, we didn't have to wait long for the proof that none of us had caused that mayhem.

I'm a bit rusty on the dates, but it couldn't have been more than a week later – probably the weekend following the disassembly of Ciaran's room – that I found myself in the kitchen with Sarah, waiting for the others to return from a night out. We had no money, Sarah and I, so we were waiting around in the hope of scrounging a few cans of beer off the other four, who surely would have garnered a few from the party for the walk home. As far as I can remember, this was the first time Ron had actually gone out anywhere with anyone else in the house.

I remember this so distinctly; I can even recall that we were listening to *The Raven* album from The Stranglers. Halfway through 'Don't Bring Harry' I could hear a clicking noise that certainly wasn't on the album the last time I'd listened to it. I paused the CD and in response to Sarah's questioning glare, I explained that I could swear I'd heard a tapping or clicking noise, and that it wasn't part of the recording. The words were barely out of my mouth when *tap, tap, tap* – pretty loud and as clear as day – came from the small fireplace beside us in the kitchen.

I don't know if you've ever noticed, but when something pretty unexpected happens, people usually don't immediately say anything. They just stare at the person with them in the hope the other person will say something logical. This was exactly the kind of exchange Sarah and I shared at that moment. Neither of us said anything. The tapping started again, a small triplet exploding in the silence.

"It's next door, cleaning out their fireplace," Sarah almost shouted. You could nearly see the relief in her face, now she'd worked out what the story was. "At half three in the morning?" I asked. In fact it was nearly a quarter to four. It hadn't actually dawned on us at the time, but there wasn't even a house on the other side of that wall – we were on the end of the row.

The tapping continued, slowly making its way up the wall; three clear taps every couple of minutes or so. Even at that stage we didn't think of the word 'ghost'. As the tapping worked its way up the wall and the across the ceiling above us, we made every kind of guess as to what it could be. We finally settled on a mouse or a rat, which had something stuck to its tail which was tapping as the rodent ran along.

Tap, tap, tap, tap, tap, tap. We both rushed out to the hallway and up the stairs. The tapping stopped abruptly. I started to get slightly uneasy. "That was strange," said Sarah. The backdoor opening and slamming shut downstairs told us my flatmates here back, so we went down to meet them, the thoughts of free beer spurring us on. A fine thought it would have been, had there actually been anyone downstairs to greet us, but the place was empty. We didn't have too much time to ponder this, as upstairs the steady staccato of tapping began once again.

Again, we tore through the hallway and up the stairs. I don't know exactly when the tapping stopped, as we made so much noise on our short journey, but when we got to the top of the stairs the house was silent again. "Sarah," I mumbled, "this just isn't right. No rat can do that." Sarah, on the other hand, wasn't even thinking of rats. She was thinking of getting the hell out of there and going home. But I wasn't going to let her leave me here on my own! We went back downstairs and right on queue, the tapping started again. With a renewed sense of bravery, we went back up the stairs – less rushed this time – and almost roared in frustration when we found the sound had stopped again. A smart rat is one thing, but one with a liking for leg pulling was just going too far. Sarah flopped down in the hallway, muttering, "I give up. This is doing my head in." I started to make my way back down the stairs, when, softly, the tapping started up once again. At that moment, we could tell that it was coming from roughly the same spot it had stopped at downstairs – right in the nearest corner of Ciaran's room. I crept back up the stairs and quietly sat down beside Sarah. Suddenly the tapping rushed to the centre of the wall. It got louder in an instant; heavier, angrier, more defined.

Then the picture on the wall started to react to the thumping, so I grabbed Sarah by the shoulder and dragged her down the stairs. We were running for our lives, leaving the lights on, the doors open and the sounds of banging from upstairs. I honestly can't say how long we were running until we met the others on their way home. I'm sure we looked like a couple of gibbering idiots.

When we got to the house, the first thing that struck me was that it was in darkness. The hall lights upstairs and downstairs had been on, but they certainly weren't anymore. The kitchen light off too, as was the stereo, which I had left on pause. It was then that it dawned on Ron, Ciaran and me that there were no insane flatmates. Something was sharing this house with us. It had wrecked Ciaran's room (which it kept like a refrigerator), it banged on walls and turned off lights – plus Bananas didn't like it.

When we got back to the house, we checked out every room as a group. At that stage Ciaran was obviously just playing it safe, as he didn't seem to be too partial to being left on his own. We had checked upstairs, and it was taken for granted no one was going back up there – up to where the thumping had been happening – so the upstairs light was switched off and we all sat down in Ron's room. The door was wide open as usual.

Here we were then, downstairs in Ron's room. Ciaran got up, went into the hallway, switched on the hall light and made his way up the stairs. I'd say he reached about the halfway mark when the hall light switched itself off with a loud click. Ciaran must have thought one of us had done it, to scare him or something, so he continued on up the stairs. What happened next was pretty quick. Ciaran's door was practically above our heads and the house, of course, was completely silent. I heard Ciaran rattling his door, then thumping on it and finally racing back down the stairs, into Ron's room and slamming the door tight behind him. "Oh sh★t! Oh sh★t! Oh sh★t! Oh sh★t!", was all we could get out of him for a few minutes. He was dazed and we couldn't get any sense out of him for a while. Whether we were imaging it or it was real, I honestly don't know, but someone was upstairs, walking around Ciaran's room.

We didn't even wait until he came to his senses. We left. Dawn was approaching, so we all made our way to the town centre and sat down at the fountain. No one talked during the journey. Everything that had made sense suddenly didn't anymore. "Tell us," Ron instructed Ciaran after we had been sitting for a few minutes. "Someone was in my room. Someone was in my room. Someone was in my room!" We got him settled and tried once more to find out what had happened. "I'm not too sure," he said. "I went upstairs … the lights went off … I made a mental note to remind you all to be more creative next time … I got to my door and I thought it was locked. I hadn't brought my keys with me though, so I knew it wasn't locked, plus when I pushed there was a bit of give. It was like there was someone inside, on the other side of the door, stopping it from opening. I was leaning right into the door when, right where my head is, it was like someone was thumping hard on the exact opposite side. There was someone in my room and they were stopping me from getting in …" A burglar is one thing, but burglars don't tend to practise squatter's rights during a job. We had checked that house from top to bottom and we were the only people in it.

There's nothing more to tell, but to be honest we never went back. We couldn't look for our money back ("I swear, the place is haunted! Give me back my money!"), but we couldn't live there either. Between then (probably mid-October) until the new term started in January, I slept in back gardens and sofas, until I could afford to rent again in the new term. That particular period of my time in Carlow is one I will never, ever forget, and it is the kind of thing I hope to never experience again. I can tell you this though: it really, honestly and truly did happen.

10

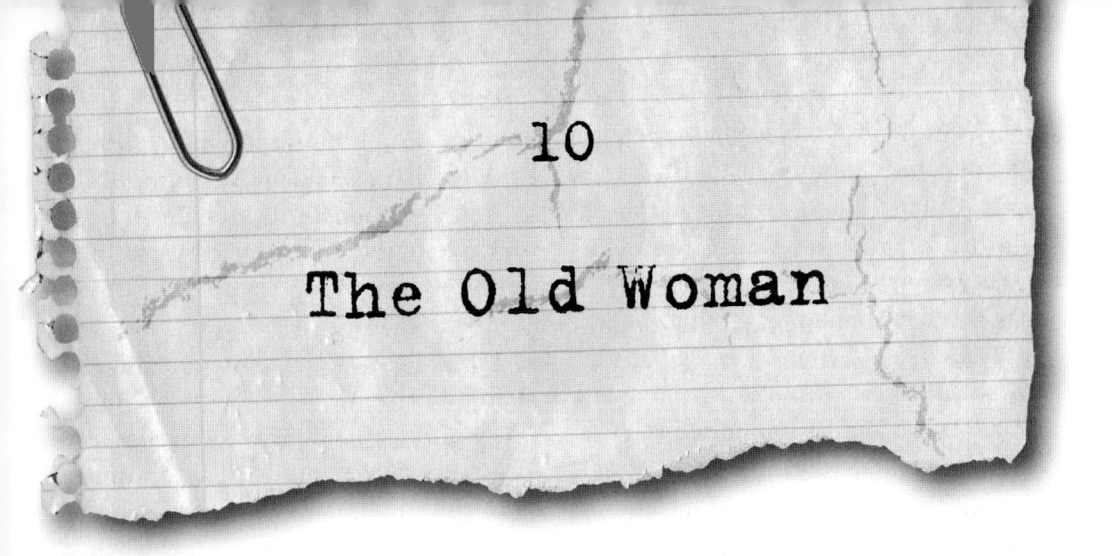

The Old Woman

THE twenty-first of August 1982 is a celebrated date in the minds of Kate and Joe. Since their marriage five years beforehand, the couple had been renting accommodation while they searched for somewhere they could permanently call home – somewhere affordable and easy to keep, yet within reach of Carlow.

It was on this day they found their ideal abode; a small two-bedroom townhouse, right slap bang in the middle of Carlow town itself. The hallway, headed by the front door and surrounded by a living room, bathroom and two bedrooms, lead into the kitchen. From there, the back door gave access to the small garden and a pathway which lead around to the front of the property. This was just what they wanted, and within a month they had moved in and started to make their new house feel like their new home.

It's hard to say when they started to feel things were slightly amiss. When it come to paranormal experiences and haunted houses, the first reaction to ghostly goings on is often the idea that it's all in the mind. People normally (and understandably) try to rationalise and explain away any apparent paranormal experiences. So it was with Kate and Joe, and though it was at least three years after moving into the small townhouse that they came to the conclusion it was haunted, things certainly seemed to have started happening within their first year of occupation.

The first 'activity' they noticed was the man in the lane. To the back of the building, running behind all the houses, was a lane. Joe first noticed a man standing directly behind their property, on the lane, looking in at them. It was the fact that this man was there most evenings, as either Joe or Kate would be closing the curtains and getting the kids off to sleep, that made the couple feel jumpy. It was hard to get a good look at him due to the bushes and branches at the bottom of the garden, but using his old telescope lens, Joe found a spot where he was concealed from this stranger. He zoned in with the lens and was amazed to find that it was in fact the previous owner of the house. Why would he be spying on his old home? Maybe he knew something about the house that Joe and Kate didn't.

Joe alternated between day and night work, so when Kate was woken at night by cutlery in the kitchen and doors opening and closing, she brushed the sounds off as Joe coming home and fell back to sleep. But then Joe moved to the dayshift, and at night he too started to hear the sounds of the backdoor opening and closing, and knives and forks rattling in the kitchen. The first time he heard it, he thought he was dreaming. A few nights later, he was woken by his wife, who hissed 'Joe! Joe! Did you hear that?'

'It's nothing,' murmured Joe in his slumber, 'It's just a dream', and off he went to sleep. The couple didn't talk of this again. Joe put it down to dreaming and Kate was convinced she was either having nightmares or imagining things. Neither even entertained the idea of a ghost.

Joe went back on the nightshift and Kate got into the habit of bringing her two kids into her room at night, comfortably wrapped up in bed beside her. Looking back, its obvious Kate was starting to feel uneasy about being in the house at night without Joe, but she didn't realise at the time that this was why she felt safer being with the kids. What she did begin to notice, though, was that her bedroom door seemed to have developed a habit of opening on its own. The door would be closed – like it would be every other night – but whenever Kate woke in the night she would find the door wide open, as far as it possibly could. 'It's the kids,' she thought, 'going to the bathroom and not closing the door.' A fine and comforting explanation it was too, until the night Kate woke just in time to see the door settling itself in its wide open stance. Both the kids were fast asleep beside her. 'That's a bit weird', she thought, closing the door carefully and firmly. When she awoke the next morning, the door was open wide once more. Yet again, Kate didn't think about this until later, but the bedroom door only acted in this strange way when she had her two children in the room with her.

It was a few more years before the couple really noticed that things were amiss. Mostly it was Kate who noticed these instances, as she was in the house more than Joe, especially at night. The most memorable in Kate's mind was when she was snuggled up in front of the fire one night, watching the TV. The show was about Joe's favourite actor, Robert De Niro, so when Kate heard the back door opening and the sound of someone into the kitchen, she called to Joe to come quickly and catch the rest of the show. On this night Joe was working late, but not on nightshift.

It was a good ten minutes before Kate realised that Joe had still not joined her, so she went down to the kitchen to find him. He wasn't there, but Kate had very clearly heard the back door open and close, and she'd heard someone come in and do something – make food, make a sandwich … something.

Joe didn't arrive back for another hour. When he did, Kate was still in the living room and she was terrified. Joe calmed his wife by telling her she probably heard sounds from outside, or from one of the kids, and she was happy to believe him.

A week or so later, Joe was having a shower. There particular make of shower was probably a pretty early example of the species, as it had a very large, complex switch, which was practically impossible to turn. Joe was halfway through his shower he heard 'Clunk!', and the water started to run cold. Absolutely freezing. Again, the word 'ghost' didn't pop into his mind. He did think it was a bit strange, but he convinced himself that somehow he turned the impossible lever himself by accident. But at that moment all Joe cared about was getting himself dried and warmed up.

There was one ultimate occurrence that seemed like the first concrete evidence that their family home was haunted. It was also a driving factor in Kate and Joe's decision to build a new home and rent out the townhouse. Admittedly the townhouse was getting too small for the growing family – which now seemed to have an extra addition.

When Kate put the kids to bed at night they would normally go off to sleep soon enough. As the children grew older (one would have been around three at this stage and the other not yet five), Kate would hear them laughing and giggling, though every now and then she would hear a quiet 'Shhh!' come from the room and the laughter would die down, before building up again after a few minutes. The first couple of times she heard this, Kate would go down to the kids' room and on the way she would hear the sound of the children hurrying back into their beds. 'They're just playing,' thought Kate.

Eventually, she tried to pry out of the kids just what they were doing, up playing when they should have been in bed. 'The old woman talks to us, Mammy', the older child said in a whisper. 'She's very funny and tells funny stories.' A chill went right up Kate's spine. But then Kate's more sceptical side kicked in with the explanation that kids have fantastic imaginations; surely that was the answer in this case.

Still, she was intrigued, and she decided to get to the bottom of this once and for all. Her first plan was to simply peer through the keyhole, which was a bit limited. She could see her youngest sitting on the ground and she could hear the kids' laughter, but couldn't really see anything else. Plan two was a bit more daring. Kate left the door of the children's bedroom open and wished them goodnight, but instead of going into the living room, she crept into her own bedroom opposite. What she saw was disconcerting to say the least. Both children were sitting on the floor, and both were looking up to the same spot above them in the air – just like they were intently listening to someone. They both laughed at the same time and both stayed quiet at the same time, but what freaked Kate out was the 'Shhh!' sound she heard, as both children were laughing loudly. If both children were laughing, then who was saying 'Shhh'? It was almost like there was another person in the room, trying to keep the children quiet so as not to the draw attention of their mother. Within seconds, Kate had the light on and was standing in the middle of the children's room. 'You scared her away, Mammy!', was all the eldest would say.

Afraid for the safety of her children (even though the old woman seem to be no threat whatsoever to her offspring), Kate told Joe everything she had witnessed when he came home later that night. One conclusion they came to was that whatever was sharing their home with them wasn't bad, but the other conclusion was that it was about time they seriously looked at what they had been thinking of for some time; building a bigger home and moving out of the townhouse. It took almost a year, but this is what they eventually did.

To this day both children, who are now well in their early thirties, maintain that they remember well the little old woman who used to lull them off to sleep with funny stories. They've never worked out just who she was though. One question did seem to be answered. The previous owner must have had similar experiences, which is probably why he was in the laneway in those early months, watching the house to see if the new occupants showed signs of having met the free tenant that had come with the little townhouse.

Our story doesn't end there. After moving, the couple rented the townhouse to numerous different people, and we tracked one of them down – a man called Mark. We asked him if he had ever experienced anything remotely paranormal that might be of interest. Indeed he did. Although he lived on his own, Mark often heard – in the dead of night as he lay in his bed – someone coming in the back door and proceeding, or so he assumed, to prepare food, as he could hear cutlery being moved around, plates being set and the general hubbub of someone in his kitchen. Initially he put it down to his imagination, then later he started getting concerned, and finally one night, armed with a stout stick, he invaded the kitchen like a ninja. Fully expecting to surprise a burglar with a culinary streak, the surprise was on Mark, as the kitchen was silent, untouched and empty.

For us, this was fantastic verification of Kate and Joe's recounts. Though Mark never experienced the old woman (granted he had no children in the house), he had experienced the same phantom sounds of someone in the kitchen and of doors opening and closing in the dead of night. Mark – obviously made of stern stuff – got used to it, and stayed there for quite a few years. Like Joe and Kate, he never felt that whatever was there was up to no good.

That little townhouse is still slap bang in the centre of Carlow, so if you happen to live there and have experienced these same things, don't worry. You aren't the first and you probably won't be the last. Do let us know all the same.

11

The Banshee

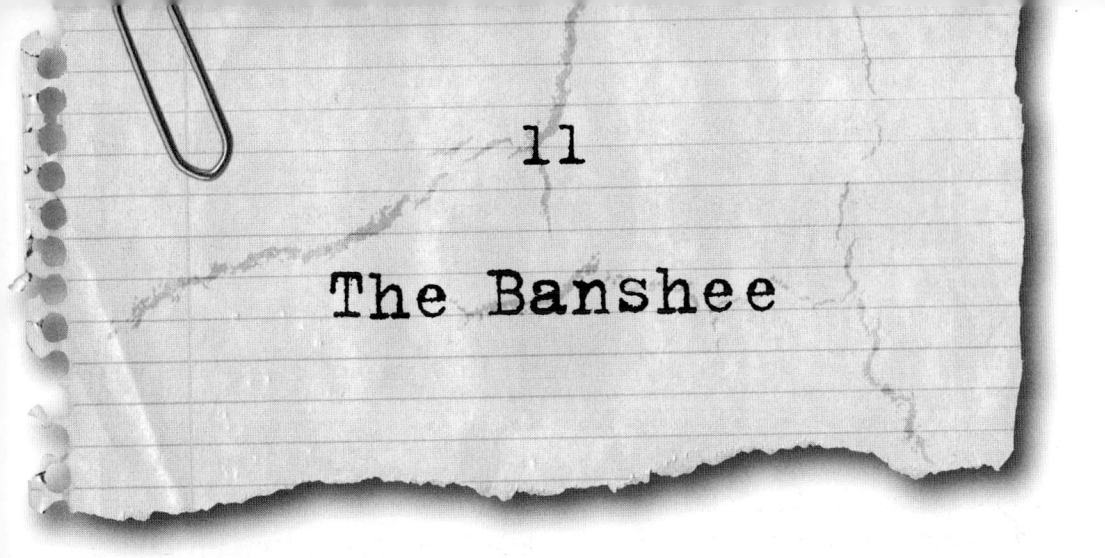

WHAT would a book of Irish ghost stories be without a chapter on the Banshee? The Banshee is the harbinger of death in Irish folklore. Many say she follows the family names of 'O' or 'Mac', but in reality, many Irish people are descended from the ancient Irish clans, regardless of their current surname, so the Banshee can appear to just about anyone. County Carlow, it seems, is quite a favourite with this much-dreaded apparition.

Some claim to have seen the Banshee, some claim only to have heard her. Either way, anyone who has had the misfortune of encountering this creature has been quite shaken by the experience. Over the course of our research, we received many, many stories about Banshees, and since many end with the expected death of a close relative, it's impossible for us to verify the truth of any of them. But still, this collection of stories clearly show the high level of belief, even in the twenty-first century, in the thing we call the Banshee.

It was a Sunday night and PJ and Anne were making their way back home. They'd been at a small social gathering in a friend's that evening, but Anne was in a rush, as it was getting late and she knew her widowed mother wouldn't sleep comfortably until she got home. 'Oh PJ! It's half twelve. Will I get a taxi home?'

'Ah it's a beautiful night Anne; let me walk you home. We'll be there in fifteen minutes.'

It was indeed a beautiful night. Dublin Street was as silent as a laneway and the gorgeous weather Carlow had been having meant the night was warm. It was perfect walking weather. But things rapidly changed, as PJ explained:

'I don't know just what I heard first. It didn't start all at once, but it all started pretty quickly; like one of those wind-up sirens they had in the wartime – not similar in sound, but in fading in and getting to a piercing scream very quickly. It was like there were three of four different people all either screaming, moaning or wailing in unison, but as soon as I began

Anne tore off around the corner and up Tullow Street. © Fran McCormack, 2010.

to realise that this sound wasn't right … well, by then it had faded away again.'

Out of the blue the Banshee had struck. The whole thing only lasted about ten seconds, although it must have seemed much longer. Neither of them had a clue what to say in the immediate aftermath and so they just looked at each other in confusion. Eventually …

'What the hell was that, PJ?' PJ, like a true Carlow man, decided that now wasn't the time to pick up his skirts and run screaming down Dublin Street. He laughed it off. 'That was two cats', he explained. 'Maybe even three.' However, barely three minutes later, as they rounded the corner of Dublin Street and Tullow Street, they heard it again. Shorter in duration this time – about half as long as before – but curiously it sounded louder. Neither of them knew where the sound had come from. Blind panic took over, as Anne tore off around the corner and up the street, hand clasped on the wrist of a very paranoid PJ. They both fled up Tullow Street.

Nothing out of the ordinary happened after this, and there were no sudden deaths in the family, but both swear blind that it happened. Of course, PJ may well have been right; it could have been cats. But just remember that story, as you walk down Dublin Street, some dark night in the future.

Our next witness, Harry, worked at Carlow railway station. It was 1990, and Harry was working the night shift. It had been belting down rain all day but it had cleared up around 8 p.m. Harry only had a few more hours of work left to do before heading home at 11 p.m. It was deep autumn and the dark nights had long taken hold, so when Harry started hearing strange noises outside his hut (which was positioned between the tracks), he knew that it would be too dark to see the cause from the window. Flicking on his flashlight as he hit the night air, Harry had a good look around the hut itself and out along the tracks. He couldn't fathom what had been making the scratching noises along the sides of the pre-fab; it had sounded almost like someone running a stone along it. 'Kids', he thought. Though the local kids rarely got up to such mischief, he was sure it was a dare of some kind.

Settling back in beside his portable gas fire, with a steaming mug of sweet tea beside him, Harry got stuck back into his newspaper. There wasn't a train due for another forty minutes and Harry fully intended to take advantage of his long break. This time, as well as hearing the scraping noises, Harry felt them, as his back was tight up against the wall. Whoever was doing it was right on the other side of the wall at that moment! 'That's a mistake,' thought Harry, as he bolted out of his seat. He tried to think

P.J., like many a Carlowman before him, decided now wasn't the time to pick up his skirts and run screaming down Dublin Street
© Fran McCormack, 2010..

up something fantastically smart-arsed to shout at the youths, as he quickly opened the door, flicked on his torch and went outside.

Immediately, he heard noises off to his far left, away from the comforting lights around the station itself. Harry was very security conscious. He couldn't carry a gun, for obvious reasons, nor would he feel safe with anything sharp, so his compromise was a sturdy Maglite torch – a pretty hefty one at that. Harry set off in the direction of the noises.

He became aware of two things almost immediately; the first that the air around him seemed to be filling up with the sounds of long, drawn-out moans and cries. It was hard to tell if it was from one voice or many, as the sounds changed so dramatically so often, but it was a sad, sick and depressing sound. As well as the sounds, he found he was looking at a small dark figure not more than ten feet away. It was dark, so clarity was an issue, but the small body seemed to rock and resonate with the cries. The Maglite cut out. Harry's heart started to pump that little bit quicker. Part of him thought this just wasn't right, but the more cynical part of his brain assured him this was just another prank. He thought it had to be a young kid; it certainly wasn't an adult anyway. He'd find out, just as soon as he got his flashlight working.

After a few swift knocks to the knee, Harry swung the lit torch towards the source of the sounds and – even though the whole episode was shorter than forty seconds in duration – Harry felt the full force of the pressure as he realised he was looking at a very old, but very small woman, who walked in circles as she keened and cried and roared. There was only one word for what he was looking at – Banshee. Any sense of care or dignity flew from Harry's head. He fell three times as he ran screaming from the tracks across to the safety of the well-lit platform. He locked himself into his hut, rang his wife and asked her to meet him at 11 p.m., and waited out the rest of his shift. Harry's mother passed away about three weeks later from a massive heart attack, and to this day, Harry swears the Banshee warned him.

Ten years earlier in Tullow, we have another account of the Banshee. This one is slightly different though. Willie worked on a Tullow farm and this particular incident took place on a warm summer evening. Summer is a busy time on the farm, and Willie had just got back from some seasonal chores. As normal, before calling it a day and getting some well-deserved supper, Willie took a walk over the fields and up to the hill where his cattle were kept. It was a clear bright evening, somewhere around 10.30 p.m. The light was just beginning to fade and the general atmosphere of the countryside made this job one which Willie looked forward to. It was the perfect time to take a leisurely stroll and plan out the tasks for the following day.

After checking the cattle, Willie made his way to the gate at the main road. From the gate, the house was in plain view and just a five or ten minute walk away. As he surveyed his surroundings, Willie noticed

A peaceful evening in Carlow railway station, but did a Banshee once lurk here? © Fran McCormack, 2010..

Carlow railway station. © Fran McCormack, 2010.

something odd about the roof of his house. What was that beside the chimney?

Intrigued, he slowly moved forward. It hadn't been windy, but it was possible that a large piece of plastic from one of the sheds that had got caught on the chimney strut. But the nearer he got, the slower he moved and the more terrified he became. By now Willie had a clear view, and it wasn't a sheet of plastic.

Hunched over and leaning against the chimney was what initially looked like an old shawl with a dirty grey mop head on top. The figure looked small, but big enough to be seen clearly. Willie froze. Whatever it was, it seemed to be roughly tugging at its dirty, clumped hair with what looked like a grotesque comb. It's hard to imagine how Willie's brain was processing this bizarre information, but he does remember thinking, 'It's a Banshee!' Except there was no sound. Nothing. No wails, no moans, no screams – just the same birds singing the same song that they had been singing all evening. It took about twenty seconds for Willie's brain to get to grips with what was going on. This was when he started screaming for his wife.

Being on a farm, Majella's first thought was that her husband had been injured, or someone or something had been killed. Tragic accidents weren't rare, especially in the summer. It was with relief, then, that she found her husband just across the fence in the field, all in one piece. This quickly gave way to growing concern, as the man was in a state of shock, mumbling and pointing up at the roof. She ran, and just as she reached her husband's side, he let out a roar of frustration. 'Willie! What's wrong?' said Majella, as she tried to calm her husband. 'Didn't you see it? Didn't you? It was there! Just as you got here …' Willie sounded like he had lost his mind.

After bringing him into the house and administering stiff whiskeys, Majella eventually coaxed Willie into telling her of the woman on the roof, of the comb and the fear. The hag had vanished as soon as Majella reached a position where she could see the roof. Willie thought he'd seen a Banshee, even though there hadn't been any noise. His wife thought he had suffered a breakdown. Nothing untoward happened after, and if it was some form of breakdown, Willie never suffered another like it again, so it's hard to say just what transpired on that rural Carlow summer's evening. 'Terrifying', is how Willie will always remember it.

The Banshee is a year-round phantom. In Leighlin one New Year's Eve, Paddy and Mary were enjoying the final hours of the holidays. Christmas had been fantastic and now they both looked forward to bringing in the New Year cosily, in front of the fire. With fifteen minutes until the final countdown of the year, Mary went to stock up on some more turf for the fire. It was a short walk from the living room, down the hall, out to the backyard and to the small shed which Paddy had packed to the brim that day with the finest turf. Mary was in a little world of her own as she filled the bucket, so the sounds she started to hear seemed to almost fade in over the quietness of the night. They quickly built in intensity. 'Oh my god!' she thought. 'Is someone hurt?' The wailing and crying was unbearable; it sounded like it was right beside her.

The back door opened, startling Mary even more, and there was Paddy, looking at her strangely. 'Are you alright Mary? Did I scare you?' he said. Mary couldn't understand this; couldn't Paddy hear what she was hearing? 'No, but that does', she replied. 'What does?' asked Paddy. Then

The backlane where locals believe the Banshee walks. © *Fran McCormack, 2010.*

the wailing stopped dead. The night was quiet again, and Paddy was looking even more concerned for his wife. 'Are you OK?' he asked again. 'No … I mean yes, I am. I must have been hearing things there for a second; I thought I'd heard someone shouting.' As she watched Paddy's reaction, she realised he hadn't heard anything. 'Don't worry about it,' she said. 'I'm fine.'

This story is a particularly sad one, because within two days, Paddy was killed in a car accident. His wife has often wondered, did the Banshee warn her, but not her husband, of his impending death?

On their way home from a night out in the outskirts of Carlow Town, Dave and Steven were enjoying the walk. It had been an exceptionally hot day and the night was warm. As they made their way down Pollerton Road, they could hear what sounded like a riot happening further along. There was crying, screaming, shouting — all echoing through the quiet night. Breaking into a run, the two lads made their way to the source of the racket, not really knowing what to expect when they got there.

Towards the corner, off on a small side street, drawn by the sharp sound of screaming, they could make out the shape of a woman. As they got closer it was obvious this woman was in great distress, on the roadway outside one of the houses. Now, not only could the two boys hear the woman screaming, but there were other sounds; mournful wails, which sounded both scary and sad at the same time.

The lady had seen them, and frantically started to run up the road calling out, 'There's something in the garden, there's something in the garden!' The wailing and crying got louder, more intense and, to a degree, closer. By the time both parties met, the woman had resorted to screaming again. The sounds seemed to be coming from the garden, suggesting that there was indeed something in there. The wailing stooped as suddenly as it had started.

The lady, Kelly, had been on her way home — she must only have been a few minutes ahead of Steven and Dave — when she passed this house and its garden. As she drew near to the entrance, that horrible wailing had started. This was obviously what the two lads had heard as they approached from further down the road. From start to finish, whatever had happened took less than a minute, so Kelly was very confused and very, very afraid. Steven and Dave were wondering if this was all some kind of ruse; perhaps a gang of muggers might appear out of the darkness. None of this made sense to anyone. Kelly ran the forty feet to her front door and let herself in and slammed the door. The first thing Dave did was take out his phone, and ring a taxi. He wasn't walking anywhere at night anymore.

12

County Carlow Tales

WE received many snippets of stories and short recounts during the writing this book, and so it's fitting that we include a chapter on County Carlow Tales. All of these stories are taken directly from our communications, with some names and places altered or removed.

Bagenalstown

'There's a house there that is said to be haunted by a man dressed in a cowboy's suit. Apparently, he appears in the house and has cursed it so that no one will ever be able to live there. I don't think any family stayed for more than fifteen years. The houses are around seventy-three years old I think. I've been living in a house close by for twelve years and a lot of people have moved in and out over that time.'

'Legend has it that many years ago, a couple lived in Bagenalstown. The husband built the house in what, at the time, would have been the middle of nowhere. He worked long hours and so he insisted on hiring a maid to keep his wife company. She grew tired of this and started having an affair. When her husband found out, he killed them both. He later grew a tumour on his face and as it rotted away, he died. They say that if you enter the house, bad things will happen and you will experience very scary things. My friends went there once and swore they would never go back. They wouldn't talk about what had happened but it was obvious that they had seen something.'

'I have no idea what happened there but that place is definitely haunted! I always get a very weird feeling when I go near it. A relation of mine was babysitting there before and the handle of the front door started going crazy. They looked out but there was no one there. As soon as they closed the door it started again. People have said that they often see a young woman walking around but no one can identify her. She just walks through the woods.'

'I remember a few years ago, in St Andrew's church in Bagenalstown, when some friends and I went in to light some candles during break. We were sitting down on the balcony and heard a woman crying. We looked around but we were the only ones there. We double checked and then ran for it!'

Carlow

'A friend of mine who lives in Castle Street has told me he has been witnessing paranormal activity in his apartment. He also heard stories about Sir Martin Morgan, who used to be a resident there back in 1930s, and who supposedly committed suicide by cutting his own throat. My friend said he has had many personal encounters with a ghost of a man with a hat, sometimes waking him up from his sleep.

He could see a dark figure standing in the corner of his small bedroom, looking at something. It then disappeared into the wall. He could occasionally hear someone's voice calling his name. I went to his apartment to do some EVPs and I caught some voices on the dictaphone in threatening tones. I also did some background into the history of Morgan's family. The family was relatively large in number, with six or seven members. William Morgan was Martin's father and they had a corn business. The story goes that Martin Morgan owed a lot of money, and because his father was reluctant to give him any, he started to drink. He was said to be famous figure in Carlow.

At the time of his suicide, it is said that Martin was in a bad state. The version my friend told me is rather scary: it's said that Martin cut his own throat, and while he was dying, his blood seeped through the ceiling to his female relative's floor. But this is only rumour. I looked up the local archive and found only the article from the week in which the suicide occurred. It only states that Mr M. Morgan was found dead due to a self-inflicted wound.

I must say that when I visited the flat, I could sense an enormous feeling of emptiness and desperation. I believe the ghost of Sir Martin Morgan still roams the place, trying to find out what has happened to him, or just lingering around due to his heavy deed. Let's hope his soul will find peace one day.'

'It was on the last Sunday of November or first Sunday of December 2004 that I saw an apparition at the entrance to the Oak Park estate. A visit to the archway was suggested to me by a local historian. I arrived at 2.30 p.m. with a camera, having been told that the arch resembled a miniature Arc de Triomphe and was well worth seeing. The historian had told me a little about the history of the estate and about its last gatekeeper. He was a friend of the Browne-Claytons (the owners of the estate) and a member of the English aristocracy. His name was Peter and he served in the British Army during the First World War. Sadly, the man suffered from profound shellshock as a result of his war service and was unable to resume his familial duties, so he kept the gate for the Browne-Claytons in the

Is there something paranormal in Castle Street? © Fran McCormack, 2010.

inter-war period. Peter would have lived in the legs of the arch; there are doors in both. He is supposed to have died just before the outbreak of the Second World War. This was all that the historian had told me about the gatekeeper.

When I arrived, I was amazed at the architecture of the arch and I began to take photos. I also considered the physical space in which Peter lived for almost twenty years. I paced the external measurements of the arch legs and was quite taken by the idea that a man had lived in two spaces of six by seven paces (as far as I remember) for that length of time. I climbed up on an adjacent wall to peer in through a window and saw a fireplace, so I assumed there would be a matching one on the other side. I passed through the arch, turned and started to examine the inside of the arch, and that's when I saw the ghost. It was standing between the legs of the arch, a little way out from the stonework, so I could see its shape and height quite clearly. The shape was semi-transparent – 'mottled' is the best word that I can think of to describe it – and had a very slight sheen, like a soap bubble. I could see no details like a face, hair or clothing, but there, no more than twenty yards in front of me, was a figure the height and shape of a man. I felt an immense chill and was surprised by the tears that began to flow from my eyes as a huge wave of sorrow overwhelmed me. I forgot the camera around my neck and all I could do was say, 'You poor soul, God help you.' I stood looking at it for about fifteen to twenty seconds until it vanished. As quick as I could, given the

An old man lived within the Archway itself.
© Fran McCormack, 2010.

The archway leading into Oak Park, Carlow where an apparition was seen.
© Fran McCormack, 2010.

shock of my experience, I took a photo of the arch from where I was still standing. There was a dark growth of lichen on the stonework and I thought that I may have discerned a pattern in it, so I wanted to check the photo when it was developed. I did not linger, as is my usual habit at such interesting places.

When I arrived home I phoned the historian and asked him if there were any reports of supernatural activity at the arch. He told me that there were some stories about a light moving between the legs of the arch at dusk or in the evening time, but nothing in broad daylight. I told him exactly what I had seen and he said that there had been no reports of such daylight occurrences. When my fiancée (later my wife) returned home some hours after the event, she found me quite shaken.

When the photos were developed there was no indication that what I had seen was a pattern of dust and lichen. I'm certain that I did see a ghost, and under superb conditions: this was not in the half-light of dusk or dawn, not something observed in movement or while I was moving, or out of the corner of my eye; nor was I aware beforehand of any supernatural or paranormal links to the estate. I've lived in four haunted houses (including one here in Carlow, but that's another story) and am grateful that I don't live in one now.'

'Forty years ago, my brother was hit and killed by a lorry. He was walking over a bridge at the time, and the lorry knocked him off the bridge and into the water. When he didn't come home that night, my mother started to worry. Jimmy was a very considerate son, and he rarely (if ever) slept anywhere but his own bed. When another day passed and there was still no sign of Jimmy, we went out and started looking. We tracked down his friends and went everywhere we could think of, but we could find no trace of him anywhere. At breakfast the following morning, my mother told us to go to the river, follow it until it passed a certain road, and then start looking deep along the left bank. When I asked why, she looked blankly at me and said, "Please just do what your mother asks you to."

We did as we were asked. We found Jimmy's body along the left bank. It had caught under roots running under the bank of the river itself. I was grief-stricken. I hadn't even considered the idea that Jimmy was dead. I thought that at worst, he'd broken with his own council and disappeared for a mad weekend somewhere. Along with this, I was confused as to just how my mother knew where to tell us to look. My mother died a few years later; she was never the same again. Before she died, she told me she was happy, as she'd see Jimmy again, just like she'd seen him the night after he died. He'd appeared in her room, arms out wide, a smile on his face, saying, "Don't worry mum, I'm fine!" I don't know what affected her more, seeing Jimmy's ghost or hearing of his death.'

Nurney

'My story happened thirty years ago on a beautiful sunny Sunday morning. I decided to take my brothers, sisters and a few of their friends for a walk around St John's Church in our village of Nurney, County Carlow. After strolling about, I stopped to take a rest, as I had to carry my youngest brother in my arms.

We all sat down. To entertain the children I went down the steep steps to the vault, knocked the door three times, and called out, "I'll meet you at midnight" (which was in a popular song by Smokie at the time). I turned to make my way up the steps, when three almighty raps came from inside the vault door. My blood ran cold and I froze on the spot. The children began to scream and I slowly made my way up the steps because my legs felt like lead. I scooped my baby brother up in my shaking arms. Our escape felt like slow motion, as the toddlers were unable to move fast through the gravel and the gate out seemed a long way off.

That morning the sleepy village was awoken by our screams. To this day I have never ventured back to the steps that lead down to the vault. I have been to two funerals during which I had to pass by and I did so with pounding heart. We talk about our experience now and again, but fortunately my little brother has no recollection, unlike his big sister, who has had many a nightmare reliving that scene.'

'This is a story I heard when I was a child living in Nurney, County Carlow. A farm worker cycled to work five days a week. His journey took him past the gates of St John's Church, down the steep hill and on to the farm about two miles further on. In summertime he encountered no problems, but come the dark winter nights, he would get off his bike at the bottom of the hill on his way home, and each time he approached the church gates, his bike would be pulled back by an invisible hand.

People didn't believe his story, until a young man reported that as he cycled to his grandparents' house (which was further up that road) his bike was pulled back with force, also by an invisible hand. Later that evening he left his grandparents' house with his brothers and a friend, and as they walked towards the village, they heard a strange noise in the distance behind them. It sounded like horses galloping at a fast pace and as they turned around they could make out the form of four black horses drawing a carriage. They threw themselves into the ditch for safety, before it disappeared as quickly as it appeared.

On the same stretch of road, a number of people have reported seeing two piercing red eyes at a gateway. The sight was described as two huge balls of fire and not human, as the distance between the eyes were too wide. People out lamping (rabbit hunting) have also seen them, and when they shine their lamp in the direction, the eyes dart away. To this day none of these mysteries have ever been solved.'